Praise for
the Meaning o

"A refreshingly spontaneous plunge into deep thought."

—*Booklist*

"While philosophy is often seen as no laughing matter, Klein's book is an argument that it can and should be. . . . It's hard to imagine a better guide." —Matt Staggs, *Biographile*

"A delightful book that is easily applicable to any stage of life. Even when explaining the underlying theories behind a quote, the author's writing is understandable for readers who have no prior philosophy background. Yet, philosophy students will also enjoy seeing the discipline applied to everyday life." —*Library Journal*

"Daniel Klein has now gifted up with a compendium of wisdom—quotes from the world's greatest philosophers, often with a light touch." —Ann LaFarge, *Hudson Valley News*

"This book not only offers a dazzling display of the superlative human thought on issues of human existence but also brings those we are not even consciously aware of into focus." —*Business Standard*

ABOUT THE AUTHOR

DANIEL KLEIN is the author of the *London Times* bestseller *Travels with Epicurus* and, with Thomas Cathcart, the *New York Times* and international bestseller *Plato and a Platypus Walk into a Bar . . .* and, most recently, *I Think, Therefore I Draw*. A graduate of Harvard in philosophy, he lives in Western Massachusetts with his wife, Freke Vuijst.

Every Time I Find the Meaning of Life, They Change It

Wisdom of the Great Philosophers
on How to Live

DANIEL KLEIN

PENGUIN BOOKS

PENGUIN BOOKS

An imprint of Penguin Random House LLC
375 Hudson Street
New York, New York 10014
penguin.com

First published in the United States of America by Penguin Books,
an imprint of Penguin Random House LLC, 2015
This edition with a new afterword published 2017

THE LIBRARY OF CONGRESS HAS CATALOGED THE
HARDCOVER EDITION AS FOLLOWS:
Klein, Daniel M., 1939–
Every time I find the meaning of life, they change it : wisdom of the great
philosophers on how to live / Daniel Klein.
pages cm
ISBN 9780143126799 (hc.)
ISBN 9780143129592 (pbk.)
1. Life. 2. Life—Quotations, maxims, etc. I. Title.
BD431.K5835 2015
128—dc23
2015015849

Printed in the United States of America

9 10

Set in Adobe Garamond Pro • Designed by Elke Sigal

For
Samara, Daniel, and Eliana
Their turn.

"Every time I find the meaning of life,

they change it."

———————

—REINHOLD NIEBUHR,

AMERICAN SOCIAL PHILOSOPHER AND THEOLOGIAN

Prologue

NOT LONG AGO WHILE PACKING AWAY SOME BOOKS, I CAME ACROSS an old notebook labeled "Pithies." Inside were short quotes from philosophers that I had jotted down, one per page, most with barely legible comments scribbled below them.

I had to smile. I had almost forgotten about this little collection of mine. The first entries bore the unmistakable blots and smudges of ink from a fountain pen—notes to myself written some fifty years ago with the pen given to me by my parents as a high school graduation gift. I must have been nineteen or twenty then and had just decided to major in philosophy in college.

The reason for that decision—and for this notebook—was that I had hoped to find some guidance from the great philosophers on how best to live my life. At the time, I didn't have a clue as to what I wanted to do after college; basically all I knew was that I didn't want to be a doctor, lawyer, or businessman, eliminations that put me in a distinct minority of my classmates. I figured studying philosophy would be just the ticket to give me direction.

About halfway through that notebook, my notations switched to ballpoint pen and my comments on the philosophers' quotes dwindled to just a few words, like "There's got to be a better way" and "Help!" The final entry was from the theologian Reinhold Niebuhr: "Every time I find the meaning of life, they change it." Under it I had scribbled, "Now you tell me!" I must have been in my midthirties when I closed the book on "Pithies."

My first reaction when I leafed through the notebook these decades later was to cringe at how naïve I had been. Did I really think I could learn how to live my life from philosophers, many of whom had lived thousands of years ago? What could I have been thinking?

Tips on how to live were few and far between in the philosophy texts I read as a student. Other questions needed to be answered first, such as, "How can we know what is true?" and, "Is there a rational basis for ethical principles?" and, "What is the meaning of 'meaning'?" After all, it made no sense to wonder about the meaning of life, mine or anybody else's, if I didn't know what "meaning" meant.

True. But in the meantime graduation was swiftly approaching, my adult life was about to begin in earnest, and I was desperate for some hints on what to do next. In the following years I dropped in and out of a couple of graduate schools of philosophy and supported myself by writing quiz questions and stunts for TV game shows, routines for stand-up comedians, and mystery novels. I also traveled a lot, usually lugging along a few philosophy books. I was still looking for ideas on how to live the best life.

Here and there, I did find some truly evocative hints and jotted them down in my increasingly tattered notebook—that is, right up to the point when it struck me that I was on a naïf's mission and I tucked "Pithies" into a box along with some old schoolbooks. That may have been around the same time I heard John Lennon famously declare, "Life is what happens to you while you are busy making other plans."

The question of how to live the best possible life had once been the central question of philosophy. It certainly had been what thinkers like Aristippus, Epicurus, Socrates, Plato, and Aristotle had foremost on their minds. And in ensuing centuries, it was the fundamental question of a great variety of philosophers, from Humanists to Deists to Existentialists.

But in recent Western philosophy, the how-to-live question has pretty much taken a backseat to the questions of epistemology (How can we know what is real and true?) and logic (What are the necessary principles of reason and rational discourse?). With a few gratifying exceptions, contemporary academic philosophers leave the whole how-to-live business to daytime TV talk show hosts, smartly dressed motivational speakers, and pop gurus who tend to favor flowing robes. According to the academics, seeking an answer to the how-to-live question is definitely not the enterprise of any self-respecting modern philosopher.

That's unfortunate, I thought, looking through my old notebook. After initially scoffing at my youthful naïveté, I now realized that those how-to-live questions were still very much alive in my mind. Sure, time had crept on and my life, with its ups and downs, had simply happened, as lives tend to do, but my appetite for philosophical ideas about life had not diminished in the least. In fact, as I look at life from the vantage point of my eighth decade, my hankering for such ideas has only increased. Late in the game as it may be, I still want to live my final years the best way I can. But more compellingly, I find myself at that stage of life when I want to give my personal history one last look-through, and I am curious to see how it measures up to fully considered ideas of a good life.

So, forty years after my last entry in "Pithies," I started jotting down new thoughts about those philosophers' quotes I had long ago copied in that notebook. And then I started collecting new quotes and noodling about them, too. Truth to tell, I was having a grand old time.

Some of these quotes sum up an entire philosophical position about how to live while others simply lob a provocative curveball in my direction, but all of them dazzle me now that I ponder them from this end of life. I am struck anew by how eloquent and inspiring great philosophers can be with just a few well-chosen words. I also realize that at my age one advantage of a concise philosophical statement is that I can still remember its beginning when I get to its end.

Personally, I have no problem with mass media gurus or motivational speakers, however they dress; I am sure they are honestly trying to answer a fundamental need in all of us. But some of the great philosophers propose truly trenchant, enduringly relevant ideas about the good life, and it would be a shame if those ideas became lost to us under a pile of pop slogans or, for that matter, under a pile of esoteric philosophical analyses of word meanings.

So here I offer my collection of concise philosophical precepts about how to live along with a personal commentary on each. Although my commentaries are meant to cast a small ray of illumination on these philosophical pronouncements, they sometimes waft off in the direction of irrelevance and self-indulgence. I have yet to find an acceptable excuse for these digressions.

Once I decided to share my Pithies with other people, I tried to figure out the best way to sequence them. Chronologically by when I jotted them down? That felt too arbitrary. By category, such as The Happy and Pleasant Life, The Meaningful or Meaningless Life, The Spiritual Life, and The Good and Just Life? The problem with the category route was that too many of the philosophers' ideas didn't fit neatly under any single heading. So in the end I went by personal association, how one idea led me, often whimsically, to another—or to put it another way, pretty much arbitrarily.

Here, then, are my Pithies, old and new, accompanied by my reflections, young and old. They may raise more questions than answers, but oh, what delicious questions they are.

> "Do not spoil what you have by desiring what you have not; remember that what you now have was once among the things you only hoped for."
>
> ....
>
> —EPICURUS, GREEK PHILOSOPHER
> (341–270 BC), HEDONIST

THIS WAS THE FIRST ENTRY IN MY OLD "PITHIES" NOTEBOOK. Hedonism appealed to me from the moment I discovered that it was a time-honored philosophy and not just a self-centered young man's daydream. But even back then I must have sensed that I was chronically cautious. I wanted to have as much fun as I could, but I didn't want to go overboard. Too scary. That is why Epicurus spoke to me: He was a *careful* hedonist.

Recently, Epicurus seems to be making a comeback with many thoughtful students. There is something appealingly New Agey about him. His aphorisms—discovered in the Vatican Library millennia after his death—read like bumper stickers written by a Zen Buddhist. Epicurus was the Prince of Pith.

In this aphorism, Epicurus is making two related points: First, desiring what we do *not* have now diminishes or even cancels out our appreciation of what we *do* have now; and second, when we take a moment to consider the outcome of actually getting that something else that we now desire, we will realize that it is just going to put us back at square one—desiring yet something else. The overall lesson is: Enjoy the present—it's as good as it gets.

Pondering outcomes is fundamental to Epicurus's general strategy for living a happy life. Not only should we think through the payoff of always desiring something more than what we have now, we should carefully think through the payoffs of *all* our desires. Like how do you think you would *really* feel if you followed your desire to bed your neighbor's wife? Figure in your guilt and scheduling complications. Still worth it? Epicurus gives teeth to the old adage, "Beware of what you desire, for you may get it."

This ancient Greek philosopher's admonition to dump our aspirations if we want to enjoy a happy life resonates with many people today—people who are starting to see the downside of always striving for more, more stuff and more achievements. The major drawback of the striving life Epicurus points out here is that there is always more to desire after a person acquires whatever it is he only recently yearned for, so he ends up with endlessly unsatisfied desire. *"My brand-new Maserati sure is neat, but what I desperately need now is a tall blonde/gorgeous Romeo to sit in the passenger seat next to me."*

An insidious manner in which we fall into the aspirations trap is in our reverence for perfectionism. We are convinced that this quality is a sign of noble character. We urge our children to be perfectionists. But the outcome of perfectionism is that we are constantly looking for ways in which we or our products could be better. A successful painter I know once told me that when she looks at her work in a gallery, she always focuses on what is missing, what would have made it better. Epicurus is right: That is a guaranteed way never to feel completely fulfilled.

Is Epicurus suggesting that ideally we go through life without any desires at all? Just be happy with what we have and what we are currently doing? Nip all our longings in the bud all the way back to sexual desire and an appetite for meatloaf? Is that the only way to lead the happiest life?

Epicurus definitely thought so and he was that rare philosopher who not only talked the talk, but walked the walk. He chose celibacy for himself because he was convinced that sex inevitably led to unhappy feelings like jealousy and boredom. And although his diet was richer than the Buddha's one grain of rice per day, Epicurus seemed happy to subsist on bread and water with an occasional lentil thrown in when he was feeling devilish. Like many philosophers, Epicurus was a man of extremes, choosing the perfect symmetry of black-and-white alternatives over nuanced subclauses of options. But unlike many philosophers, he really did practice his purist philosophy in his own life.

My dog, Snookers, is a natural hedonist and one reason for that is that he does not hold a long view of his life. He does not desist from eating a yummy cache of overripe mackerel he finds in our compost heap because it will cause him stomach cramps a few hours later. What's "later" to Snookers? He simply enjoys each moment without analyzing future outcomes, poor guy. That little doggie does not have a clue of how to go about weighing his options, let alone making tradeoffs. We humans are far better equipped for that.

Or are we? Modern psychology raises some serious questions about our ability to foresee gratifying outcomes. In his remarkable book *Stumbling on Happiness*, Harvard psychologist Daniel Gilbert demonstrates that we humans have a lousy record at predicting what will make us happy, from with whom we pair off to where we live. In most cases, Gilbert says, we would have the same chance of finding happiness by flipping a coin as we do by carefully deliberating our options.

Still, Epicurus's Zenlike lesson does hit home for me, in fact more now than it did when I first read it. Although generally I do not drift away from the present by desiring more, frequently I do drift away from the present by fantasizing about what's coming up next. I now realize that I have spent much of my life thinking about "What's next?" While eating dinner, I will start thinking about what book I am going to read or what movie I am going to watch *after* dinner. Meantime, I am not focusing on my lovely mouthful of mashed potatoes.

In fact, "What's next?" has been the leitmotif of my life. As a child, I constantly thought about what my life would be when I grew up; later, about what life I would lead when I graduated from college. On and on. Thus have I diluted my life. As Ralph Waldo Emerson wrote, "We are always getting ready to live, but never living."

A fundamental tenet of many of the world's major religions is that life on Earth is but a trifling stage on the way to Real Life, the life in the eternal hereafter. Our mission here is to prepare for that heavenly life, mostly to make sure we qualify for it. Other than that, our mundane lives do not mean a whole lot. So what we have here is a life of perpetual "What's next?" Every moment of our earthly lives is focused on the *next* life.

Modern evangelists hit this point repeatedly in their sermons and homilies. Preaches Pastor Rick Warren: "Life on earth is just the dress rehearsal before the real production. You will spend far more time on the other side of death—eternity—than you will here. Earth is the staging area, the preschool, the try-out of your life in eternity. It is the practice workout before the actual game; the warm-up lap before the race begins. This life is preparation for the next."

My personal "What's next?" compulsion is far less comprehensive than the one Pastor Warren advertises, and it definitely lacks the Great Hereafter payoff he promises. And without this payoff, my habit makes no sense at all.

But I don't want to brood about that now: Spending time regretting anything is another sure way of missing what is right in front of me. Furthermore, at my age and with my nonotherworldly worldview, I'm pretty sure I know what's next.

I REMEMBER WHAT I WAS FEELING WHEN I WROTE THIS ONE down: Challenged! Dared! The 1960s were dawning along with their ethos of radical freedom and I felt tested by it. Suddenly, Epicurus's cautious hedonism felt like a timid man's bluff. *My* bluff.

Aristippus was the real deal, an unbridled Hedonist. None of that Epicurean parsing of pleasures. No if/then dithering about the lurking dangers and unwelcome outcomes of acting impulsively. No admonishments to be careful in taking your pleasures lest you hurt or upset someone else. And clearly, no finger wagging in the name of Virtue.

No, this ancient Greek philosopher urges us to get down and dirty. He wants us to be hedonists in the sense that word is used today: pure pleasure seekers. Sensualists! *Animals!*

Is Aristippus talking about that fancy sports car *complete* with the hot blonde/gorgeous Romeo in the passenger seat?

You betcha, if that is your "keenest" pleasure.

How about orgies?

Go for it, says Aristippus.

It even appears that the "art of life" could include some passing masochism if one agrees with the original sadomasochist, the Marquis de Sade, who wrote, "It is always by way of pain that one arrives at pleasure."

Yes, this is definitely starting to feel like a scary dare, yet I cannot help but feel a certain admiration for the purity, so to speak, of Aristippus's hedonism. He does not hedge on his "pure-pleasure-is-the-only-purpose-of-life" philosophy. He forces me to ask myself if there legitimately can be such a thing as a half-hedonist. And if so, what is the other half? A wuss?

It took courage for Aristippus to break completely with the teachings of his honored mentor, Socrates, who advocated a good and just life over a life of undisciplined frolicking. Apparently it also took some bitchiness on Aristippus's part—that is, if accounts of his gossipy opus, *On the Luxury of the Ancient Greeks*, are to be trusted. (Many scholars do not believe Aristippus wrote it.) In that *National Enquirer*–like history, Aristippus gleefully spills the beans on Plato's romps with boy lovers. From some perspectives, Plato's romps may not appear to be the behavior of a good and just Athenian, but, of course, ethical norms have a way of changing over time—just as philosophies of life do.

As a guide to seeking out life's pleasures, Aristippus flips Epicurus's basic premise of hedonism upside down. Whereas Epicurus would have us rein in our desires and aspirations so that we can get the most pleasure out of what is right in front of us, Aristippus urges us to actively manipulate what is in front of us in order to maximize our pleasure. Man is the architect of his own pleasure dome.

Judging by Aristippus's own life, one way he manipulated what was in front of him was by traveling—from his birthplace, Cyrene (in ancient Libya), to Athens to Rhodes and back to Cyrene. In his day, this was equivalent to a world cruise. The way it worked for him seems to have been that when, say, he tired of the view from his terrace in Athens or of the arms of his favorite Athenian courtesan, the glamorous Lais, he packed his bags.

Another way Aristippus managed to make over his immediate environment was by shopping. Evidently, the man adored luxury. He was an early advocate of the "he-who-dies-with-the-most-toys-wins" school of hedonism. The way Aristippus could afford his self-indulgences was by charging his philosophy students tuition, a practice that both Socrates and Plato, early proponents of free access to information, abhorred. Epicurus would have strongly disapproved, too, starting with his precept that striving to achieve absolutely anything, even if it is only toys, is a sure way to miss out on an *angst*-free life. And for Epicurus, an *angst*-free life was the only truly happy one.

When I was in my late twenties living on the Greek island of

Hydra, I witnessed another anxiety that Aristippus's anything-goes hedonism can stir up. During that time, I often hung out with another expatriate, Habib, a wealthy Iranian who had been brought up in Paris. Habib was what was known as a *fils a pappa*—a wayward young man who is such an embarrassment to his wealthy father that he is supplied with a tidy sum to just go away. Habib had the time and money, not to mention the good looks, to do pretty much anything he wanted. Furthermore, Habib was not in the least inhibited by conventional norms of acceptable behavior. In short, he had the potential to enjoy Aristippus's perfect life.

But Habib was overwhelmed by all his options. Why spend the night with Sophia when spending the night with Katrina might be even more sensational? Why smoke some opium when getting drunk on ouzo might be more fun? Or what about both? Time and again, I would find him on the terrace of Loulou's taverna in a paralyzing dither. Often, I had to suppress a chuckle over his befuddling embarrassment of riches, but for Habib it was no laughing matter. Hedonism made him anxious.

Still, I definitely find something refreshing about Aristippus's unequivocal, no-nonsense brand of hedonism. Among other things, it is not so cerebral as other philosophers' brands and for good reason: Aristippus was convinced that intellectual pleasures do not begin to measure up to sensual pleasures.

My dog, Snookers, would agree with Aristippus—that is, if Snookers knew what agreement was. Yet therein lies the reason why I, personally, cannot subscribe to Aristippus's art of life: I simply am not comfortable seeing myself as an animal with only animal appetites. Don't get me wrong: I love and admire animals, Snookers in particular, but my human consciousness just cannot be denied. I guess it took Aristippus to force me to admit to myself just how anthropocentric I am.

So is my resolute humanness the only reason that I have never indulged in an orgy, appealing as that fantasy might be? Or, for that matter, is it the reason I never set out to acquire a closet full of Armani blazers?

I have to admit that, try as I might, I could never completely will away my ingrained anxieties—anxieties very different from Habib's, but just as inhibiting. For example, I worry that at an orgy I would find it hard to breathe under all those frenetic naked bodies. And then there's my chronic laziness. Would I really have to get out of bed before dawn to make big-bucks deals on the Tokyo Stock Exchange? These apprehensions are undoubtedly what really account for my demurring from orgies and from demanding, money-driven labor. Not exactly a philosophical position, but there it is.

> "Genetic engineering and nanotechnology will
> abolish suffering in all sentient life. This project is
> ambitious but technically feasible. It is also
> instrumentally rational and ethically mandatory."
>
> ....
>
> —DAVID PEARCE, BRITISH PHILOSOPHER
> (1960–), HEDONIST

THINKING ABOUT HEDONISM AS AN OLD GUY WHO HAS LIVED
through some extraordinary "If-it-feels-good, it-*is*-good" periods of
American life, I had to wonder if contemporary philosophers had
been keeping up with our modern-day *dolce vita*. Well, it turns out
they have—and then some.

A bright young philosophy student I know put me on to a
visionary contemporary philosopher and cult figure named David
Pearce, author of the popular online book, *The Hedonistic Imperative*.
Pearce is a certifiable mind-blower. He forces me to ask myself if there
is anything more valuable in life than feeling sensationally good all of
the time. So into my recently resumed notebook Mr. Pearce went.

He starts out by taking his basic premises from two traditional
philosophers, Epicurus and Jeremy Bentham, the eighteenth-century
British social philosopher. From Epicurus comes the tenet that the

happiest life is one of *ataraxia*—freedom from fear—and of *aponia*—the absence of pain. And from Bentham comes the Utilitarian idea that all actions should be guided by the principle of providing the greatest happiness for the greatest number of people. Pearce believes not only that both of these ideals are self-evident, but also that they put a demand on us to do absolutely whatever is possible to make happiness universal.

What Pearce adds to the hedonistic tradition is an up-to-date (and beyond) technical program for how to get there—how to create an entire world of perpetually pain-free and depression-free people. The way he sees it, "Our descendants will be animated by gradients of genetically pre-programmed well-being that are orders of magnitude richer than today's peak experiences." He is talking smiley faces everywhere, 24/7.

It may all sound like science fiction, but Pearce is an expert on nanotechnology (constructing devices, such as electronic circuits, out of single atoms and molecules), genetic engineering, and designer drugs. Apparently, while I have been quietly drinking vodka tonics, biomedicine has been busy concocting an astounding number of novel methods for what they call the "neuromodulation of mood." These include transcranial magnetic stimulation, central nervous system prostheses, and electrical neurostimulation implants.

Not only does Pearce say that it is "ethically mandatory" to "eradicate suffering in all sentient life," he is confident this is within our technological reach. Epicurus had his blueprint for avoiding pain, and Pearce is merely giving us a new and advanced blueprint for doing the same thing—High Tech Hedonism.

But I do wonder if Pearce's program is possible given certain limitations of the human condition. What I know about nanotechnology would fit in a molecule, but I have read a bit about the cultural history of altered consciousness.

When Indian and Ceylonese tea first came to England in the mid–seventeenth century, imbibers wrote rhapsodic essays about how deliriously happy this "hypnotic" made them. Some said they could not sleep for days afterward, so wired and besotted were they by one cup of the stuff. According to one eighteenth-century commentator, tea was so habit-forming that it did not take long for all of Great Britain to develop a serious tea addiction. So why, then, does your average, twenty-first-century London matron who consumes five cups of tea daily seem so sedate, so very far from ecstatic? Because they had stronger tea back in the old days?

That's unlikely. It is probably because being high/stoned/drunk is always relative to "normal" consciousness, both normal for an individual and normal for the culture in which he lives. Over the centuries, virtually everyone in England has developed "tea consciousness." That is not because absolutely everyone there drinks tea, but because a sufficient number did and do and their resulting consciousness became the norm. The culture born of tea consciousness informs daily language and personal interactions; it becomes part of the process of successful socialization. If virtually everyone regularly ate magic mushrooms, "magic-mushroom consciousness" would eventually become our norm. If you spent a long period of time in a magic-mushroom-consuming community, you would soon realize that their language and its commonly understood referents are markedly different from those of talk around your home dinner table. The mushroom people are speaking the language of psychedelic consciousness and, over time, you would very likely acquire that consciousness and language whether or not you were a mushroom eater yourself. Similarly, computers and social media have changed the consciousness of our culture, affecting—without our fully realizing it—our accepted ideas of a normal attention span and personal intimacy.

The end result is that eventually tea (or mushroom or computer) consciousness simply begins to feel like normal consciousness, not higher or better consciousness. The feeling of being high is in its contrast to everyday consciousness; the only way we can feel high is for there to be something to feel higher *than*. In order for that London matron to feel more euphoric, she would have to try something else, say a glass or two of scotch at teatime; but, of course, that would only work for a limited amount of time because after a while "scotch consciousness" would become her normal consciousness. It is worth noting that people who are drunk all day every day do not strike me as a particularly happy lot.

One time in the 1960s when my friend Tom Cathcart and I were experimenting with LSD, Tom suddenly stopped gazing around rapturously and announced soberly, "Geez, you can always get higher, can't you?"

The answer, sadly, is yes, we can always get higher. The reason we can always get higher is that we can only possess one consciousness at a time, and whatever that consciousness happens to be can always be transcended. Somewhere deep inside we all know this, but people who have gone on psychedelic trips are keenly aware of it. They have watched themselves jump from one level of consciousness—and the euphoric feelings connected to that consciousness—to another. They have even watched themselves *watching* themselves jump from one level of consciousness to another, which is a particularly dizzying quality of consciousness unto itself. As it happens, the limited size of our brains stops us in our transcendental tracks before we get within hailing distance of the end of this hall of mirrors.

The critical point is that knowing we can always get higher can be a real downer. It informs us that we are never going to reach the ultimate point of happiness because there *is* no ultimate point of happiness. There is always a higher mountain thataway. For someone seeking ultimate bliss, this is a sobering thought. It all starts to feel futile. But not to worry: Soon enough the mountain on which we are currently sitting becomes our new normal consciousness and our level of happiness feels more or less the way it always has.

Experimental psychologists refer to this as our "happiness set point." Their research suggests that inducing happy feelings cannot have lasting effects on our sense of well-being. Their "hedonic treadmill" thesis says that we constantly habituate ourselves to acquired levels of happiness and so we simply return to our original baseline level of feeling.

Here is where the "set-point" theory starts to both intrigue and confuse me. If everyone eventually returns to some baseline feeling, why are some people's baselines higher than others'? And why are some cultures' baselines higher than others'?

Different societies clearly do have different general levels of well-being. The overall self-evaluated happiness of the people in southern Europe is significantly higher than that of the people in northern Europe. The Italians and Greeks laugh and smile more than the Germans and Dutch. They also take more pleasure in simple routines, like eating long lunches and sitting around and chatting. (This may very well be the root cause of the north-south economic tensions involving the euro currency; the northern Europeans think the southerners are lazy, while the southerners think the northerners don't know how to live a good life.) While teaching for a semester in Rome, I read a newspaper survey of how the average Roman occupied his day: He spent a lot more time eating, napping, and chewing the fat than his counterpart in Berlin. My favorite statistic was that the average Roman spent an hour and a half each day listening to music. That must be hedonism at its most sublime.

In any event, Pearce will have none of this set-point theory. He points out that depressed people who take Prozac feel a lot better than they did before taking the antidepressant and most continue to feel that way as long as they take the pill. What is more, these people are fully conscious that they feel better than when they were depressed and are grateful for it. So, asks Pearce, why shouldn't we all take pills or, for that matter, get electrical neurostimulation implants that continuously make us feel good, that make us, as Pearce says, "feel better than simply well"? He insists that our society and our psychotherapists have established the base point of feeling good and happy way too low. He writes, "[I]f we recalibrate our typical emotional set-point, then the greatest happiness principle can be implemented far more successfully than in the wildest dreams of Bentham."

But Pearce doesn't give the full story here. A significant number of people on Prozac need to increase their dosage continually to stay free of depression. Could that be because after a while their medicated happiness set point starts to feel drab, even depressing? Wouldn't that happen with neurostimulation implants, too? Pearce doesn't fully answer the relativity-of-well-being problem.

Okay, one more question about the genuine possibility of feeling terrific all the time. Taking a quick survey of the most ecstatic moments in my life, I would have to put sexual experiences at the top of the list. Now would I want all of my life to be one long orgasm? Alas, I think not, and I do not believe this is my age talking. Not only would this lifelong orgasm start to get strenuous after a month or two, it would probably get monotonous. I would start to miss other, less intense feelings.

Pearce is way ahead of me on this. He claims that his project would work it out so that we could calibrate our feelings to exactly the way we want them at any given moment. So while we are in one synthetically produced mood we will predetermine our next synthetically produced mood. *I think I'll go from some orgiastic ecstasy to a brief interlude of beatitude.*

Even if Pearce's feel-good utopia actually is possible in the not-too-distant future, the question remains: Is it a good idea?

Most people don't think so, starting with their aversion to what they see as its artificiality. They say that if you only feel happy as a result of some transcranial magnetic stimulation, it is not *real* happiness. In fact, it is not the real *you* who feels happy. Incidentally, this distinguishes most people from most rats, who apparently do not mind if their happiness is artificially induced. In an often-cited rodent behavior study, rats kept pressing a lever that zapped their cranial pleasure center right up until they conked out, having skipped eating, drinking, and sleeping in order to keep their pleasure pulsing away nonstop.

Humans are less consistent on the artificial happiness issue. For example, most anti-artificial-happiness folks tend to make an exception for a couple of shots of bourbon at the end of a long day just to "loosen up." Ditto for the occasional tranquilizer, joint, or can of Red Bull in the middle of the afternoon for a little pick-me-up. But transcranial magnetic stimulation? No way. That is simply unnatural.

The most compelling critique of artificially induced emotions I have come across is in George Saunders's short story "Escape from Spiderhead." In this futuristic fable, the protagonist is a subject in experiments with mind- and emotion-altering drugs that are pumped into his system via a "MobiPak" surgically implanted to his lower back. In one experiment, he is placed in a room with a woman named Heather whom he initially finds unappealing; but once he is pumped with a finely titrated love/sex drug, he finds her irresistible. Heather is also so dosed. They make passionate love. He is convinced that she is his perfect match, the answer to his dreams. Later, he is chemically weaned from her to the point of indifference. And then he is presented with a new woman, Rachel, and the same sequence is repeated, complete with his sense of this woman being his one true love. Says the protagonist:

"Soon my memory of the perfect taste of Heather's mouth was being overwritten by the current taste of Rachel's mouth, so much more the taste I now desired. I was feeling unprecedented emotions, even though those unprecedented emotions were (I discerned somewhere in my consciousness) exactly the same emotions I had felt earlier, for that now unworthy-seeming vessel Heather. Rachel was, I mean to say, *it*."

Sublime love, total delight in finding one's long-desired soul mate, is thus reduced to drops of a drug. And once the experimental subject knows that, strong as his current feelings are, he realizes that ultimately his love is meaningless. (Of course, some readers may see Saunders's tale as wicked commentary on the undrugged, but nonetheless fickle, human heart.)

Deep down most of us ultimately prefer everyday reality to artificial reality. The late Harvard philosopher Robert Nozick offered a simple thought experiment he called the Experience Machine for sorting out how we stand on the everyday versus artificial reality choice: "Suppose there were an experience machine that would give you any experience you desired. Super duper neuro-psychologists could stimulate your brain so that you would think and feel you were writing a great novel, or making a friend, or reading an interesting book. All the time you would be floating in a tank, with electrodes attached to your brain. Should you plug into this machine for life, preprogramming your life experiences? [. . .] Of course, while in the tank you won't know that you're there; you'll think that it's all actually happening[. . . .] Would you plug in?"

It turns out that most people who tried this imaginary scenario on for size decided that in the end, they wouldn't plug in, because they want to actually *do* certain things, not just have the "sense" of doing them. People simply feel a basic allegiance to everyday reality. They see it as the one true reality.

But Pearce has little patience with the artificial pleasure antagonists. He likes to point out that when anesthesia was introduced to operating rooms in the mid–nineteenth century, there was an outcry against its perverseness. One obstetrician who adamantly refused to use "gas therapy" for painful childbirth wrote that labor pains were "a most desirable, salutatory, and conservative manifestation of the life force." And anesthesia was not a manifestation of the life force—not natural—so it was not good. Pearce's anecdote is a good reminder of our innate stubbornness when faced with new methods, but I don't think it completely addresses our preference for "real" everyday life.

A powerful argument against Pearce's brave new world is inspired by the novel *Brave New World*. In Aldous Huxley's fictional futuristic society, citizens get blissed out on the drug "soma," which, as Huxley wryly puts it, has "all of the benefits of Christianity and alcohol without their defects." Well, *one* defect: People on soma become dull, unimaginative, and lazy. Critics of Pearce worry that this is just the kind of society his universal hedonism would produce: meatheads from coast to coast.

Basically, this is a "no pain, no gain" argument for preserving human emotions like frustration, competitiveness, and general malaise. Such emotions are the mother of invention, progress, and a long view of life—say a view of life that worries about global climate change or exhausting our natural resources. Absent these emotions, we would be happy to just sit still and be deliriously happy while the planet came to a standstill.

But it turns out to be more complicated than that. According to many psychologists, the happier people get, the better are their friendships, marriages, work performance, health, and income. In short, no pain, *more* gain.

Another point of view on the "no pain" problem comes from that perennially pessimistic philosopher, Arthur Schopenhauer, who believed in a sort of "no pain, *more* pain" scenario. He thought a Pearcelike contented world would end up making us more depressed than ever. In his *Studies in Pessimism*, he wrote: "If the world were a paradise of luxury and ease, a land flowing with milk and honey, where every Jack obtained his Jill at once and without any difficulty, men would either die of boredom or hang themselves."

Maybe there really is something deeply existential at risk in Pearce's feel-good utopia. Perhaps we need to endure some pain in order to become fully human—like the pain that comes from consciousness of our mortality, consciousness of our inevitable limitations and failures, and consciousness of all that is mysterious about existence itself. Without this consciousness, we might be nothing more than cheery animals. Our lives would be existentially shallow. But then again, if we are feeling absolutely hunky-dory all the time, who cares about all that existential stuff?

Sometimes Pearce's argument for the perfectly happy man seems to me like hedonism gone mad. It feels like a vision of la-la land, a place where we are no longer genuinely human. But for that very reason, I think this young philosopher is absolutely brilliant. More than any other philosopher I know of, Pearce compels us to examine the foundation of hedonism. Is pleasure all we really want in our lives?

That must be pretty close to the first question for any philosophy of life.

> "Life oscillates like a pendulum, back and forth
> between pain and boredom."
>
> ....
>
> —ARTHUR SCHOPENHAUER, GERMAN PHILOSOPHER
> (1788–1860), METAPHYSICIAN AND ETHICIST

OKAY, I ADMIT IT: EVERY ONCE IN A WHILE I DO HUNGER FOR A good dose of pessimism, especially when I am up against a rough patch in my life. It is callously comforting to think that life stinks for everyone when it happens to stink for me. At times like this, who better to turn to than Mr. Melancholia himself, Arthur Schopenhauer? I cannot remember exactly when I copied this one down into my notebook, but I bet it was during one of my deep-in-the-dumps periods.

Hard as it is to believe, Schopenhauer is considered a hedonist because he acknowledged happiness as life's ultimate goal. He just thought it was virtually impossible to get there. Like Epicurus, he defined happiness and pleasure as the absence of fear and pain. Also like Epicurus, Schopenhauer believed that reducing our expectations was the primary way to beat the blues. The German philosopher put it bluntly: "The safest way of not being very miserable is not to expect to be very happy." You have to love those words "very miserable"; Schopenhauer could not be content with simply saying "unhappy" as Epicurus did.

From there, Schopenhauer's philosophy continues downhill, *way* downhill. In his tome *The World as Will and Representation*, he writes, "The shortness of life, so often lamented, may be the best thing about it." In *The Vanity of Existence*, he writes, "Human life must be some kind of mistake. The truth of this will be sufficiently obvious if we only remember that man is a compound of needs and necessities hard to satisfy; and that even when they are satisfied, all he obtains is a state of painlessness. . . . This is direct proof that existence has no real value in itself." And then, of course, there is his *uber*-dreary "pendulum" dictum. We get the idea.

At some point during a solitary young manhood rife with failure— nobody bought his books, no university would take him on as a teacher—Schopenhauer came upon the earliest Western-language translations of the Upanishads (also known as the *Oupenkhat*), a Buddhism-inspired Hindu text. In these mystical/metaphysical writings, he found a deep resonance with his own philosophy, although the Eastern philosophy ultimately bears a more positive outlook. The Upanishads suggest that through detachment and resignation a person may be able to experience a peaceful accep-tance of life, an attitude that Schopenhauer gradually began to adopt toward the end of his life. In this latter period, he wrote that the Upanishads "has been the consolation of my life and will be of my death." For Schopenhauer, admitting that he felt some consolation was roughly equivalent to anyone else shouting, "Whoopee!"

These Eastern texts appear to have significantly changed Schopenhauer's life, although, ironically, in a very mundane way. In his sixties, he published a book titled *Parerga and Paralipomena* (Greek for "Appendices and Omissions"), much of it a rehash of his pessimistic philosophy, but a good part of it an assortment of catchy aphorisms. Lines like: "Mostly it is loss which teaches us about the worth of things," and, "Each day is a little life: every waking and rising a little birth, every fresh morning a little youth, every going to rest and sleep a little death," and, "Honor has not to be won; it must only not be lost."

Yup, a lot of it is fairly banal stuff, yet many people found these maxims as charming and winning as Epicurus's aphorisms. In terms of Schopenhauer's development as a writer, *Parerga and Paralipomena*'s format of bite-size precepts owes a great deal to the Eastern religious books he had read, particularly the Brahma Sutras, a Vedanta/Hindu volume of easy-to-swallow aphorisms.

Parerga and Paralipomena became a runaway bestseller. Suddenly Mr. Melancholia became the toast of the town, complete with fetching girlfriends, grand parties, and fan mail. His brand of pessimistic hedonism had found its audience. People saw something terribly romantic in all his *sturm und drang*, especially if they could read it in catchy, short bits while taking a hansom cab to Berlin's fashionable Café Bauer.

The twentieth-century philosopher Bertrand Russell, by all accounts a generally charitable man, thought that Schopenhauer was a consummate hypocrite. Wrote Russell: "He habitually dined well, at a good restaurant; he had many trivial love-affairs, which were sensual but not passionate; he was exceedingly quarrelsome and unusually avaricious. . . . It is difficult to believe that a man who was profoundly convinced of the virtue of asceticism and resignation would never have made any attempt to embody his convictions in his practice."

In writing this, Russell could be accused of making an *ad hominem* criticism of Schopenhauer's philosophy. But then again, Schopenhauer's philosophy is ultimately about an attitude toward life and, among other things, an attitude toward life is a psychological phenomenon. Pessimism is something people feel and it colors the way they see things. This feeling may give birth to a philosophy, but in the end neither the feeling nor the philosophy can be proven. Modern psychologists would look at Schopenhauer's life and see a man with a serious self-esteem problem who, after he became a big shot, overcame his depression and became a party animal. I get Russell's point; that born-again party animal business makes it harder for me to take Schopenhauer's abject world-weariness seriously.

In any event, at this point in my life I can never take Schopenhauer's pessimism to heart for very long. Even in the worst of times, something usually comes along that *spritzes* me with hope—some small, everyday event that unexpectedly revives my appetite for life.

Toward the end of Woody Allen's movie *Hannah and Her Sisters*, the character Mickey (played by Allen) delivers a long monologue about a time in his life when he was so overcome by Schopenhauerian pessimism that he attempted suicide. His attempt failed and he started roaming the streets of New York, then impulsively ducked into a movie theater where the Marx Brothers' *Duck Soup* was playing. Recounts Mickey:

"I just needed a moment to gather my thoughts and, and be logical and put the world back into rational perspective. I went upstairs to the balcony, and I sat down, and, you know, the movie was a film that I'd seen many times in my life since I was a kid, and I always loved it. And, you know, I'm watching these people up on the screen and I started getting hooked on the film. And I started to feel, how can you even think of killing yourself? I mean isn't it so stupid? I mean, look at all the people up there on the screen. You know, they're real funny, and what if the worst *is* true.

"What if there's no God, and you only go around once and that's it. Well, you know, don't you want to be part of the experience? . . . And then, I started to sit back, and I actually began to enjoy myself."

Mickey/Woody's epiphany reminds me of Oscar Wilde's marvelously pithy, "We are all in the gutter, but some of us are looking at the stars."

> "There is but one truly serious philosophical problem
> and that is suicide. Judging whether life is or is not
> worth living amounts to answering the fundamental
> question of philosophy. All the rest—whether or not
> the world has three dimensions, whether the mind has
> nine or twelve categories—comes afterwards."
>
> ....
>
> —ALBERT CAMUS, FRENCH PHILOSOPHER
> (1913–1960), EXISTENTIALIST

EXCUSE ME IF I LIE DOWN ON THE COUCH FOR A SPELL, BUT I CAN never read this Camus pronouncement sitting up. Indeed, I was lying in a gutter of gloom with no stars in sight when I copied this one into my notebook, but to this day I still believe that Camus's dictum is absolutely right and absolutely essential.

If the fundamental question of philosophy is "What is the meaning of life?" then we have to begin by tackling the problem of whether or not our individual lives are worth living—and therein will lie our answer. (For those who sincerely believe that the fundamental question of philosophy is whether the mind has nine or twelve categories, feel free to stop here.)

The power of Camus's statement begins with the fact that in the world of living creatures, only human beings are able to contemplate and carry out suicide as a conscious decision. To those quibblers who believe that salmon commit suicide via their perilous swim back to their spawning pools, I can only say that I am pretty sure salmon do not cash it all in as the result of deep philosophical reflection. If a human is conscious and mobile and reasonably resourceful, he can freely decide to kill himself and then do it.

Most of us have never genuinely considered this possibility. We know rationally that suicide is an option, but we may not have ever truly contemplated it—not focused on it with head and heart while sitting alone in a dimly lit room. It is terrifying.

Before going on, it is important to note that Camus omits the psychological perspective on the suicide question, namely that a mentally ill person could be in such deep psychological pain that suicide appears to be the only way out, the only relief. Most psychiatrists would say that such people actually do have other options, such as medication and psychotherapy. More significantly, they would also say that suicidal people are not rational by definition—that *anybody* who commits suicide acts irrationally. Camus, of course, would say that genuinely contemplating suicide can be supremely rational.

I know a man whose eldest child killed herself in her late twenties. For a long time, this young woman had been withdrawing from society, spending most of her time alone in the woods. Her family and friends worried about her, but she did not respond to their pleas that she seek psychiatric help. She did not leave a note telling why she killed herself. Many people deeply grieved her loss. Her father was inconsolable and left his hometown for several years. When he returned, he appeared more at peace. He said to a friend, "It's not only that I wish she was still alive, I wish she had found a reason to live." Bravely and profoundly, he had found his way to the source of the tragedy.

For me, the most compelling and horrifying description of an individual contemplating suicide is found in Graham Greene's extraordinary personal essay "The Revolver in the Corner Cupboard." Beset by unmitigated feelings of emptiness in his teenage years, Greene would steal off with his brother's pistol to Berkhamsted Common and there play Russian roulette: He would insert a single bullet, spin the chamber, press the gun to his head, and pull the trigger. When there was only a click (and there was every time he tried it), he would experience an overwhelming feeling of happiness. "It was as if a light had been turned on . . . I felt that life contained an infinite number of possibilities."

Camus certainly would not recommend Russian roulette. For one thing, it ultimately puts the all-important existential decision of whether to live into the hands of the fates. But Greene's act dramatically shows how confronting suicide can enable a person to *own* his ultimate reason for living, whatever that may be. Once a person is absolutely clear on the fact that it is his choice whether to continue living, he has arrived at the point where he either has a reason for living or does not. Equivocation is over. And choosing to remain alive—choosing life—is the prelude to creating one's own meaning of life. We choose to remain alive for a *reason,* even if that reason is no more specific than, "I just don't want to die."

When Camus wrote in *The Stranger,* "You will never live if you are looking for the meaning of life," he was suggesting this same point from a different angle. The meaning of life is not something we *look for,* it is something we *create.* And by contemplating suicide, we can be fully present at our own creation.

> "My first act of free will shall be to believe in free will."
>
> ....
>
> —WILLIAM JAMES, AMERICAN PHILOSOPHER
>
> (1842–1910), PRAGMATIST

Of course, before I choose the meaning of my life, it would probably be a good idea to ask whether I have a free and independent will with which to do so.

If Epicurus was the Prince of Pith, William James was its CEO. In the above statement, he gives the most succinct and efficient argument I know of for adopting a belief in free will.

The Free Will versus Determinism debate has been raging in philosophy since the days of Aristotle, but recently cutting-edge discoveries in brain science have purportedly given the determinists an upper hand in the debate. Brain maps reveal an awful lot of cause-and-effect going on inside our skulls, and decision-making is no exception. These scientists claim that what we call making a free decision is just bouncing atoms doing their random thing.

I definitely need to think about that, but first a pause for my favorite philosophy headline of all time: "Templeton Uses Its Wealth to Debase Philosophy."

The story that followed told of a $4.4 million grant from the Templeton Foundation to come up with a definitive answer to the Free Will Question. The recipient, the philosophy department of Florida State University, and its leading philosopher, Alfred Mele, accepted the grant in a heartbeat. It goes without saying that this kind of money had never before been bestowed upon any philosophy department anywhere. No one had ever coughed up even a few thousand to focus on the philosophical question of, "Why are there things that exist rather than nothing?" So why is Florida State's windfall considered a tool of debasement?

Follow the money. The billionaire CEO of the Templeton Foundation, John Templeton, is a devout Fundamentalist Christian who also contributed over $5 million to the University of California to study the impact of near-death experiences on the likelihood of an afterlife. Even to a nonphilosopher, this may appear as if Mr. Templeton is trying to buy confirmations of his fondest beliefs, roughly akin to the pharmaceutical giant GlaxoSmithKline, makers of the antidepressant Paxil, donating $1.2 million to a university research laboratory to study effective treatments for depression. (GlaxoSmithKline did, in fact, do that, and the resulting experiments determined that drugs like Paxil did, in fact, do the trick.)

I do have to wonder what Templeton thinks he is getting for his money. Does he think that if a philosopher or brain scientist can build a coherent argument that the afterlife exists, that means it *really* must exist and therefore he can die peacefully? It is almost touching how much faith Templeton has in academics, even if those academics might conceivably be influenced by the size of their paychecks.

But why, at this particular time, did Templeton put so much money into the Free Will versus Determinism debate?

Undoubtedly because the brain science determinists are currently prevailing, and if they are right, it has some terrifying implications for issues of moral responsibility. If a person did not have free will, how could he be held accountable for the bad things he did? The bouncing atoms made him do it. This prospect is particularly disturbing to a devout Christian like Mr. Templeton. What would determinism do to the concepts of sin and redemption? Furthermore, implicit in the brain scientists' argument is that everything in the universe is reducible to matter. Mind is reducible to the activity of brain cells, so ultimately only the brain cells are real. In philosophical terms, these scientists are monists—they reject the dualism of people who believed in both material and immaterial things like minds and immortal souls. Monism is definitely not on Templeton's wish list.

And now, after that word from the sponsor, back to the Free Will versus Determinism debate as it affects a person who is about to set out on the existentialist task of willfully creating the meaning of his own life.

I am always drawn to the no-nonsense pragmatism of William

James. His goal is to make philosophy relevant to real life, and on the question of free will he does so wonderfully and with his usual wit: "My first act of free will shall be to believe in free will."

His underlying point is that there is no objective and scientific way to prove the existence of a free will. You can't see one, even with an X-ray machine (discovered during James's lifetime). Therefore, accepting its existence is akin to an act of faith; it is something we can *choose* to believe in. Herein lies James's little gag: Choosing to believe in *anything* is an act of will; without a will, no choices exist. In fact, how could you "choose" *not* to believe in free will? In that case, some determinant must have forced the choice. So there is something wonderfully circular about James's free will declaration; he is already accepting the idea of a free will by the very act of making a choice; in this instance, the choice to believe in a free will.

The pragmatic piece of James's decision is that believing in a free will feels intuitive. It is fundamental to what feeling human is all about; it is basic to being an "I." That is, right up until we find it useful or comforting to believe that uncontrollable forces determine our actions. Then we are back in "the devil made me do it" territory. *Ladies and gentlemen of the jury, please consider my traumatic childhood when you pass judgment on me—my upbringing made me do it.* And then there is my all-time favorite, "the Twinkie Defense"—*All that sugar in the Twinkie I ate made me pull the trigger*—from an actual San Francisco murder trial.

I wonder how a person's behavior would change if he thought

his every choice *was* determined. How would he go about letting things happen determinably? And who, exactly, would be making the decision to let things happen that way? This simply does not seem a practical or gratifying way to get through a day, let alone a lifetime.

But William James was not a dewy-eyed philosopher who was totally content with his pragmatic argument for acting as though free will existed. (I, on the other hand, am perfectly content with this argument.) Some years later, lecturing to students at Harvard Divinity School, James explored the free will question in a heady and wonderfully imaginative way, employing my favorite philosophical method, the thought experiment.

He begins by asking, "What is meant by saying that my choice of which way to walk home after the lecture is ambiguous and matter of chance? . . . It means that both Divinity Avenue and Oxford Street are called [to mind as alternatives] but only one, and that one *either* one, shall be chosen."

And then begins his wild thought experiment:

"Imagine that I first walk through Divinity Avenue, and then imagine that the powers governing the universe annihilate ten minutes of time with all that it contained, and set me back at the door of this hall just as I was before the choice was made. Imagine then that, everything else being the same, I now make a different choice and traverse Oxford Street. You, as passive spectators, look on and see the two alternative universes—one of them with me walking through Divinity Avenue in it, the other with the same me walking through Oxford Street. Now, if you are determinists you believe one of these universes to have been from eternity impossible: you believe it to have been impossible because of the intrinsic irrationality or accidentally somewhere involved in it. But looking outwardly at these universes, can you say which is the impossible and accidental one, and which the rational and necessary one? I doubt if the most ironclad determinist among you could have the slightest glimmer of light on this point. In other words, either universe—after the fact and once there—would, to our means of observation and understanding, appear just as rational as the other."

It's a tough-to-grasp argument, but it's a honey.

> "Existence precedes essence."
>
> ....
>
> —JEAN-PAUL SARTRE, FRENCH PHILOSOPHER
> (1905–1980), EXISTENTIALIST

WHEN I FIRST READ SARTRE AND HIS FELLOW EXISTENTIALIST, Albert Camus, I was smitten. This was philosophy about life, about finding meaning and about how to conduct oneself. Sure, some of it was heady and abstract. (One fellow student told me that he tried reading Sartre's *Being and Nothingness*, but his eyes glazed over when he got to nothingness.) Yet this was the kind of philosophy I had been looking for from the start.

If there was a contest for the shortest statement that sums up an entire philosophical position, Sartre's above three-worder would win—or at least tie with Berkeley's *"Esse est percipi"* ("to be is to be perceived"). It is the foundation upon which modern Existentialism was built.

Sartre is saying that unlike objects in the world—say, my toaster—human beings cannot be defined by their properties. A toaster is created to toast breadstuff; the capacity to toast is the toaster's purpose and essence. But we humans can generate and change our fundamental properties and purposes along the way, so it does not make sense to say we have some immutable, defining essence. First, we exist, and next, we create ourselves. This is not something my toaster could do even if it wanted to.

Of course, Sartre does not mean we can self-create our physical properties. I cannot will myself to be tall. Nor can I will myself to be Moroccan-born. But the important stuff is mine to determine, like how exactly I want to live, what I want to do with my limited time on Earth, what I am willing to die for—the qualities that fundamentally make me an individual. All of those are up for grabs. My grabs.

Sartre and his Existentialist coffeemates, Camus and Simone de Beauvoir, dispensed with the free-will-versus-determinism conundrum in a William Jamesean way: Their first act of free will was simply to declare that existence precedes essence. Now down to business.

Sartre is not merely *describing* this potential that is unique to human beings, he is *exhorting* us to embrace it and with it our responsibility for whom we become. If we sidestep this human capacity, we abandon our very being. We allow ourselves to become just another object.

Sartre's catalogue of the various ways we unthinkingly manage to turn ourselves into objects—to act as if our essence precedes our existence—is daunting. We slough off the responsibility to create ourselves by shrugging and claiming, "That's just the way I am." "I smoke because I have an addictive personality—that's just the kind of guy I am." Or, "I believe in the God of Abraham because my mother told me to—that's just the way I grew up." Another dodge we try on ourselves is to identify our essential natures with a predetermined role, say that of wife. "I am a wife—that is simply my identity." Of course, if we *choose* the identity of "wife," that's perfectly authentic, but if we think we are predefined by that identity—that it is our immutable essential nature—we are turning ourselves into an object.

According to Sartre, we are historically prone to thinking of ourselves as objects due to the Judeo-Christian credo that God stamped us with our essence from the get-go; it is His prerogative. So to think that we are able to stamp ourselves is a sacrilege. But the main reason we keep ducking the responsibility of self-creation is that it is super scary. If I am the master of my fate and my fate does not turn out so well, I have no one to blame but myself.

When all is said and done, this Existentialist precept resonates with me more than any other philosophy of life I know. The idea that life's meaning is not something to look for but something to create myself *feels* right to me. In fact, it seems absolutely essential.

JUST AS I WAS REVELING IN THE EUPHORIA OF EXISTENTIAL FREEDOM,
a college friend handed me her copy of Nietzsche's *Thus Spake Zarathustra*. It was her way of saying to me, "Think again, buster."

Nietzsche agreed that we create our own lives, but he main-
tained that not *all* chosen meanings of life are created equal. Some
meanings are inherently better than others—better by a critical
order of magnitude.

Before reading Nietzsche, I had been thinking that all things
considered, I would probably be happiest with an easygoing life.
No high drama, just the simple pleasures—a kind of low-key
American variation of Epicureanism. So maybe I should design my
life along the lines of that nice fellow, Frank Busby, in my old
hometown. Busby is happy, generous, a splendid father and
husband, has a steady job he enjoys, and is a member in good
standing of the volunteer fire department. Sounded like a good life
to me. And, after all, I do get to create any life I want, right?

Not so fast, spake Nietzsche. Some of us have the capacity to live in a way that goes far beyond the ordinary, and it is incumbent upon us to reach for such a life, to fully engage in what he calls "life affirmation."

Maybe Busby is content to live a simple and comfortable life following the accepted rules and mores of religion and society, but Nietzsche calls Busby a weakling for choosing to live that way. Actually, Nietzsche says, Busby didn't *choose* his life at all; he just accepted the script society gave him and lives accordingly. He cannot shake off his "herd instinct" because, to begin with, he has no real consciousness of the fact that he is part of the herd. Busby cannot honestly face up to who he is and what he deeply feels. As a result, he is never fully alive—he never truly lives.

So do I really want to live out my days like Busby?

Friedrich Nietzsche's essays, books, and aphorisms cover a great deal of territory and much of that territory has been subject to a considerable variety of interpretations by philosophers and psychologists who followed after him. But on the question of how a man should live his life, Nietzsche unequivocally advocates a radical conception of "To thine own self be true."

To begin, a man who aspires to this kind of personal honesty must throw off all interpretations of himself that depend on anything that supposedly transcends his life, such as a god or a soul. Man exists here in this world, so that must be his point of departure.

Staying free from his psychological and intellectual inheritance will be a continual struggle for him, an ever-lurking danger.

But what is the nature of this true self that the daring man seeks? Nietzsche believed that what this man will find deep inside is not very pretty. He wrote that if I am diligent, in my depths I will discover my "madman," "immoralist," "buffoon," and "criminal." Only then, Nietzsche said, will I finally tune in on something of value. Then I will be ready to actualize my true nature. And it does not look a bit like Frank Busby's.

The contemporary philosopher Thomas Nagel lays out the Nietzschean alternatives cogently in this line: "The point is . . . to live one's life in the full complexity of what one is, which is something much darker, more contradictory, more of a maelstrom of impulses and passions, of cruelty, ecstasy, and madness, than is apparent to the civilized being who glides on the surface and fits smoothly into the world."

Yes, this definitely sounds like a dangerous way to live.

In the 1960s and 1970s, the idea of finding one's true self and giving it full expression was very much in the air. In pursuit of this goal, many of us went into psychoanalysis or group therapy, practiced Transcendental Meditation, imbibed mind-expanding drugs, and engaged in talk marathons during which we tried to strip away all artifice, all delusion, all the bullshit we habitually told one another. I remember that many a romance and friendship was wrecked along the way.

Timothy Leary, a pioneer in psychedelic drugs and the leading guru of this period, exhorted us to "Turn on, tune in, and drop out." His message had a decidedly Nietzschean motif, as in these words in his guided meditation "How to Operate Your Brain": "Throughout human history, as our species has faced the frightening, terrorizing fact that we do not know who we are, or where we are going in this ocean of chaos, it has been the authorities—the political, the religious, the educational authorities—who attempted to comfort us by giving us order, rules, regulations, informing—forming in our minds—their view of reality. To think for yourself you must question authority and learn how to put yourself in a state of vulnerable open-mindedness, chaotic, confused vulnerability to inform yourself."

Many of us determined that our "true selves" had been stifled by our conformist society. We quit our jobs and schools and took to the road. We discovered that what we really wanted deep down was to be free spirits, answerable to no one. We followed every impulse, even if it was mad, immoral, outrageous, or criminal. Some of us carried around tattered paperback editions of Nietzsche's *Thus Spake Zarathustra* in our jeans' pockets.

In those years, I tried rather clumsily to straddle the worlds of conformity and nonconformity. I would earn a living conventionally for a few years, then take off for parts unknown for a long spell. In one employed period, I earned a living by working for a TV game show by day, but by night and on weekends, I engaged in "alternative" pursuits. It was not always an easy mix, but it did have its merry moments.

One Monday, I turned up at my office for the game show *Reach for the Stars* with a large residue of LSD still rambling through my nervous system. My job at the show was to make up stunts for contestants to perform—stunts like, "Pull on this pair of size-fifty jockey shorts over your pants; you now have thirty seconds to stuff your underpants with these ten balloons without breaking them." That Monday, I had a remarkably productive day at the office.

Trying to juggle these two ways of living often ended up with my behaving hypocritically, but it did have the advantage of giving me perspective on a new kind of conformity I saw developing—"hippie" conformity. One day, as I was walking to the subway on my way to *Reach for the Stars*, a fellow my age approached me. I was wearing my workday chinos and checked shirt; he was decked out in full hippie regalia—well-worn bell bottom jeans, tie-dyed T-shirt, and a long feather tucked into a dazzlingly colored headband. I admired his entire presentation of himself—it seemed joyful and daring. Then he said, "Let me have a dollar, brother!" I didn't feel like giving him a dollar, so I didn't. He then gave me a patronizing scowl and snarled, "Just like I figured—you're uptight!"

Perhaps he was right, I really was uptight, but it struck me that in adopting the hippie binary ethic of "uptight" versus "with it," this guy was as conformist as any 1950s suburbanite. He saw himself as a member of the "with it" in-group and me as a member of the "uptight" out-group. It was high school all over again, but instead of wearing a varsity football sweatshirt, the in-group guy was wearing a tie-dyed T.

In the end, many of us, both hip and not so hip, had unwittingly stopped struggling with all the contradictions that still raged deep inside us. We had become as complacent with the mores of our new "groovy" lives as Busby is with his. Perhaps for some of us our lives were still dangerous in terms of punishing policemen and disapproving parents, but we were still dodging the dangerousness of our inner inconsistencies and of our existential dread. A true Nietzschean man confronts these every moment of his life. For example, rare was the hippie who ever admitted to himself that one of his inner selves—just a tiny one—might be happy living in a comfy home with a spouse, two kids, and a dog.

During this same period, "self-actualization" became a cottage industry in psychotherapy. The maverick therapist Abraham Maslow wrote, "[T]he desire for self-fulfillment is the desire to become more and more what one is, to become everything that one is capable of becoming." He believed "self-actualization" should be the ultimate goal of all therapy. Nietzsche's prescription for leading a dangerous but authentic life had been transformed into a way to feel good about oneself, to be one happy guy.

I have to admit that in the past few decades, I don't seem to have much interest in ferreting out my deepest self. After a while, that pursuit began to feel futile. There always seemed to be another self hiding beneath the one I had just found—selves all the way down. Or, as a friend of mine once quipped, "We turned out to be superficial to the core." I know that Nietzsche would admonish me to deal with it, to keep wrestling with this endless regression of internal contradictions, but these days I would rather spend my time making peace with who, for better and for worse, I have become. In the end, instead of aspiring to be an *ubermensch*, I simply aspire to be a *mensch*. I opt for the tranquil hedonism of Epicurus's Garden. Which is to say, I am probably a lot like Frank Busby.

> "Nature, with her customary beneficence, has ordained
> that man shall not learn how to live until the reasons for
> living are stolen from him, that he shall find no enjoyment
> until he has become incapable of vivid pleasure."
>
> ....
>
> —GIACOMO LEOPARDI, ITALIAN POET AND PHILOSOPHER
> (1798–1837), PESSIMIST

WHAT IF IT TURNS OUT THAT ARISTIPPIAN HEDONISM REALLY *IS* the way to go, but I'm now too old to relish it? What an awful thought! And leave it to Giacomo Leopardi, the renowned early-nineteenth-century Italian poet and philosopher, to nail this predicament with his usual grim gusto. I only came upon the above quote recently—in other words, after it was too late to do anything about it. In a passing moment of masochism, I wrote it down anyhow.

Although noble-born and privately tutored by conservative Catholic priests, Leopardi evolved into the high priest of nihilism and pessimism. For him, life was a nonstop bummer. Leopardi's philosophy can be summed up in the old adage, "Things can only get so bad . . . and then they get worse."

He saw all of life as if it were the denouement of an old Russian curse. Like, "You should find a *ruble* on the sidewalk but be too arthritic to lean over and pick it up." Or, one of my favorites, "May they find a thousand new cures for you *each year.*"

This Italian saw life as a grand joke: We are handed a life full of promise, but all we end up with is one disappointment after another. Ha, ha.

Philosophical pessimism is not merely an emotional attitude toward life, it is a rebuke of the very notion of progress. It is a reproof of the Western ethos of earnestly pursuing a more perfect world—all those ideologies that propel social and political movements, not to mention every self-improvement strategy we've ever tried. In a world full of trap doors that willy-nilly drop us into frustration and despair, working for progress is a joke—and a sick joke, at that. On top of that, philosophical pessimism takes a pot shot at the optimism born of faith in a beneficent, well-meaning god.

Yet Leopardi is a pessimist with an upbeat kicker: Once we fully acknowledge that life is doomed to perpetual disappointment, we can have a good laugh about it, and that turns out to be liberating. That is when the fun begins in an ironic, bittersweet sort of way. His outlook resembles that of the 1960s pop anthem of existential futility, "Is That All There Is?" As Peggy Lee sang, "If that's all there is my friends, then let's keep dancing / Let's break out the booze and have a ball."

Wrote Leopardi, "He who has the courage to laugh is master of the world, much like he who is prepared to die." And in his *Manual of Practical Philosophy*, he took a dig at the pursuit of happiness: "If all you seek from something is pleasure, you'll never find it. All you will feel is *noia* [existential boredom], often disgust. To feel pleasure in any act or activity, you have to pursue some end other than pleasure."

To put it another way, the pursuit of happiness is a guaranteed dead end, but if you give up on that pursuit, you just might have some wild and crazy times out there.

In Leopardi's line about there being no enjoyment available to us until we are incapable of having pleasure, he certainly strikes a nerve in this old guy. Yes, Signor Leopardi, many of those "vivid pleasures" have seeped away with the years. These days, the song is sweeter than ever, but it is getting harder and harder to hear. *Literally.* Yet every once in a while in the wee hours, lying on the living room sofa with my wife as we listen to Jacques Brel sing his achingly beautiful *"Ne Me Quitte Pas"* at a volume audible to my dimmed hearing, I often believe that I have found a peace that transcends those vivid pleasures.

And yet I have to admit that at other times I can't help wondering: What if I had pushed the hedonism envelope further when all my senses were still in perfect condition? Would my one and only life have been richer?

Such thinking can only lead to regret. And on that subject, I am with Woody Allen: "My one regret in life is that I am not someone else."

> "The goods of the mind are at least as important
> as the goods of the body."
>
> ....
>
> —BERTRAND RUSSELL, BRITISH PHILOSOPHER
> (1872–1970), LOGICIAN AND HUMANIST

THANKS, BERTIE. RIGHT ABOUT NOW I NEEDED THAT. TOO OFTEN it is easy to forget the unique pleasures available at this end of life, and one of them is surely quiet and unhurried thinking. I only came across this quote recently and immediately plunked it into my Pithies notebook.

I have always gotten a kick out of the way Russell puts things. It is frequently so very, very Oxbridge British mixed with regular-folks talk. Like that word "goods"—that's the stuff you find in your local shop, right?

One of the things Russell is doing in this statement is aligning himself with the long line of philosophers who believe that thinking supplies us with one of life's greatest pleasures. When the nineteenth-century social philosopher John Stuart Mill laid down the Greatest Happiness Principle as the basis of Utilitarianism, he stressed that purely animal pleasures don't make the grade. Wrote Mill, "It is better to be a human being dissatisfied than a pig satisfied; better to be Socrates dissatisfied than a fool satisfied." For him, there are lower pleasures and higher pleasures, with intellectual fun being the high-quality stuff. Call it Cerebral Hedonism. *I think, therefore I feel good.*

Russell is not just saying that thinking is a *prerequisite* for leading a gratifying life as Socrates meant when he said, "The unexamined life is not worth living." Rather, Russell believes that examining life is one of the essential treats that make life worth living. He thinks that thinking is delightful in itself, possibly even better than a roll in the hay. It is worth noting that unlike the celibate Epicurus, Russell had a very active sex life both within and without marriage, so he does not speak naïvely about the "goods of the body." There are just *good* goods and then there are *very* good goods—the kind you pick up while sitting alone in your easy chair puzzling over philosophical questions.

It is philosophical thinking that Russell finds particularly life-enriching. In his lovely and highly accessible essay "The Value of Philosophy," Russell demonstrates how confronting the big questions enlarges us. Questions like: "Has the universe any unity of plan or purpose, or is it a fortuitous concourse of atoms? Is consciousness a permanent part of the universe, giving hope of indefinite growth in wisdom, or is it a transitory accident on a small planet on which life must ultimately become impossible? Are good and evil of importance to the universe or only to man?"

Russell readily admits that such questions are ultimately unanswerable. He says that "those questions which are already capable of definite answers are placed in the sciences, while those only to which, at present, no definite answer can be given, remain to form the residue which is called philosophy." It is that residue of unanswerable questions that he finds so stimulating and inspiring.

Russell knows full well that "many men . . . are inclined to doubt whether philosophy is anything better than innocent but useless trifling, hair-splitting distinctions, and controversies on matters concerning which knowledge is impossible."

My father, a scientist, was one of those men. Half a century ago, when I informed him that I had decided to major in philosophy, he muttered something about "mental masturbation." In those days, any kind of masturbation—mental or manual—was generally considered unwholesome, even depraved. For one thing, it was antisocial; for another, it did not produce anything useful. Dad, a child of the Depression, valued usefulness above all. He was definitely not a hedonist. For him, studying philosophy was simply a waste of time.

Russell believed just the opposite. He wrote, "The man who has no tincture of philosophy goes through life imprisoned in the prejudices derived from common sense, from the habitual beliefs of his age or his nation, and from convictions which have grown up in his mind without the co-operation or consent of his deliberate reason. To such a man the world tends to become definite, finite, obvious;

common objects rouse no questions, and unfamiliar possibilities are contemptuously rejected. . . . [But Philosophy] keeps alive our sense of wonder by showing familiar things in an unfamiliar aspect."

I particularly love those last two lines. Among other things, they contain the most powerful antidote to boredom I know of.

A few weeks ago I was engaging in the most banal and potentially boring of enterprises—sitting for over an hour in the waiting room of my doctor's office where I had come for a routine check-up. I had failed to bring along a book and not a single magazine on the waiting room table enticed me. (Alas, I have arrived at the point in life where my once-favorite waiting room periodical, *People* magazine, features people I have never heard of.)

Soon I found myself wondering about the concept of "waiting." Clearly, it always has a goal—the end of the waiting, the thing anticipated. It also implies delay—hanging around doing nothing until something of importance happens, namely the thing delayed. In this sense, it suggests some sort of "dead time," either those periods when we naturally are not conscious, like sleep, or, from the point of view of a Buddhist, those awake times when we do not remind ourselves to be conscious, to be fully mindful of our existence.

I then wondered if every language has a word and concept for "waiting." Does it exist in the languages of primitive societies where every individual human endeavor is experienced as part of a group enterprise? In such a society would what we call "waiting"— say, waiting for a turn to take a handful of porridge—be seen as an activity itself, an *active* part of the group dynamic? Does anything like what I experience as waiting exist for Snookers? Does he have some primal sense of waiting when he hangs around his food dish as his dinnertime approaches?

Believe me, I am well aware that none of my waiting-room musings was profound in the least. But, minor as they were, they *were* philosophical: They proceeded from wonder and led to further wonder. A thing most ordinary—hanging out in a waiting room—had been looked at from a perspective that was new for me. Also, I had incidentally been doing some phenomenology—the early-twentieth-century philosophical discipline of reflecting on the structures of consciousness and its contents. Yup, I had just been doing some amateur phenomenology of "human waiting."

I am sure my father would have seen all this as just more mental masturbation, and I definitely get his point. My wonderings certainly never really get me anything or anywhere. But they do happen to make me feel more alive, so I am grateful for the capacity to wonder that was nurtured by reading philosophers. What's more, those wonderings in the waiting room did help pass the time.

Toward the end of this essay, Russell offers a nod to classical Greek hedonism when he says that "the philosophic life is calm and free." Epicurus believed that life does not get any better than that; a tranquil life is brimful of pleasure. But then Russell raises his sights even higher for the life of the philosophical mind. He concludes that "through the greatness of the universe which philosophy contemplates, the mind also is rendered great, and becomes capable of that union with the universe which constitutes its highest good."

It almost sounds like Russell sees philosophy as a religion. Maybe I have finally found a congregation I would happily join—that is, if they would have me as a member.

> "It is one of the blessings of old friends
> that you can afford to be stupid with them."
>
> ....
>
> —RALPH WALDO EMERSON, AMERICAN PHILOSOPHER
> (1803–1882), TRANSCENDENTALIST

I COPIED THIS ONE INTO MY NOTEBOOK WHILE I WAS STILL IN college, long before I was old enough to have an old friend. But I may have been prescient: At the time I had just made a new friend, a fellow philosophy major named Tom Cathcart who has remained my closest friend for going on fifty-seven years now.

Through the ages, an impressive number of philosophers—from hedonists to transcendentalists—have rated friendship as life's greatest pleasure. Not sex, not extreme sports, not even coming up with an original philosophical insight—but simply having a very good friend. Epicurus and Aristotle thought so, so did Montaigne and Bacon, Santayana and James. It is a long and impressive list. Given that doing philosophy is one of the most introverted occupations imaginable, it is fascinating that these folks valued companionship so much. Perhaps it takes being a solitary person to fully appreciate the pleasures of friendship.

Of course, there are some philosophers who hold a cynical view of friendship. The French master of maxims, François de La Roche-foucauld (1613–1680), wrote, "What men have called friendship is only a social arrangement, a mutual adjustment of interests, an interchange of services given and received; it is, in sum, simply a business from which those involved propose to derive a steady profit for their own self-love."

Yes, we all have had relationships like that—relationships that turned out to be more about manipulation than companionship, more about being treated as a means to an end than as an end itself. But true, open, and trusting relationships exist also. I know this to be true in my most valued friendships and I have the incomparable privilege of being married to someone I trust with my life.

An insidious form of La Rochefoucauld's cynical appraisal of friendship is in the air lately. It is called "setting boundaries," and mental health tipsters from Dr. Phil to the editors of *Psychology Today* swear by it. The idea is that you should consciously set limits on what you are willing to do with and for your loved ones; that way you will not get riled or burned in your relationships. They tell us to set boundaries on what we are willing to sacrifice for our friends, what we will tolerate in their behavior, even what we talk about with them. That way we will have healthier, more peaceful friendships.

In *Psychology Today*'s "10 Tips for Setting Boundaries and Feeling Better," they list as number 5: "Understand the laws of reciprocity—The best way to receive support, love and feelings of satisfaction and contentment is to lend it out, offer your help, donate your time, reach out to someone you love."

In other words, base your relationships on the commercial model of *quid pro quo*: If you do for me, I'll do for you. It sounds like La Rochefoucauld's "social arrangement, a mutual adjustment of interests, an interchange of services given and received." Is that what we want to mean by "friendship"?

Recently, a friend of mine told me that she had worked out a tidy and workable formula for sustaining her marriage even though she and her husband had been growing further and further apart for many years. She said they no longer shared the same values; in fact, they saw just about everything in the world so differently that it was impossible to have anything but contentious conversations with each other. But they had three children and she felt it was incumbent upon her to keep the marriage going. Hence her formula, which consisted of setting extreme boundaries on what could and could not be discussed and at what points they would temporarily withdraw from each other. It sounded to me like something one might read in a business manual on how to keep antagonistic employees from gouging each other's eyes out. My friend asked me what I thought of her formula and I replied, honestly, that it sounded good to me, as long as she was willing to completely give up on genuine intimacy.

Surprisingly, my friend was taken aback by my comment. She had not thought about her situation in those terms. She had been living without genuine closeness for so long that she seemed to have forgotten how much she actually valued it and longed for it. And no "boundaries" formula was going to change that; indeed, it would only codify a way to live without the possibility of closeness. She realized that what she ultimately needed to decide was if she was willing to live without intimacy for the rest of her life.

But back to Emerson's thoughts about the joys of an old friendship. I know whereof he speaks. Tom and I have kept in close touch—daily touch since the advent of email—over the decades. Once or twice a year, we go off together for a few days, stay in a B&B or hotel, and basically just hang out. We talk. We go to a movie. We eat out. We talk some more. It is a treat and a privilege.

Over these years, we have gone through the rough passages of our respective lives with each other's counsel and support. The good parts, too, of course. And some of our long, heady discussions on philosophical topics have taught me more than I learned in any classroom. But if I were to pick out the most ecstatic times we have shared, those would be the occasions when we were pickled with goofiness, when we reduced each other to giggling fools. We trust each other enough to be able to be seriously stupid together. Total dumbos. And in the midst of so much laughter, there are sometimes moments when time seems to stop for a delirious rendezvous with the Eternal Now.

> "Our language has wisely sensed the two sides
> of being alone. It has created the word loneliness
> to express the pain of being alone. And it has created
> the word solitude to express the glory of being alone."
>
> ....
>
> —PAUL TILLICH, THEOLOGIAN
> (1886–1965)

AS MUCH AS I CHERISH THE JOYS OF GENUINE COMPANIONSHIP, I do love the glory of solitude. This is a pleasure that has deepened for me with age. Often, solitude can fill me with peacefulness and a simple gratitude for being alive. Sitting alone in the back of our little house on a summer's day, a field of long grass and wildflowers before me, I revel in the mere act of breathing in and breathing out.

On her trips to the vegetable garden, my wife sometimes offers me an amused smile as she passes by. Once, a few years ago, she asked me if I was thinking deep thoughts out there in my chair. I happily confessed the truth: I didn't have a single thought in my head, deep or shallow. That was a substantial part of what made it so delightful.

Indulging in solitude is certainly selfish, but I do not think it is egotistical. I don't sit there congratulating myself on being me.

If I congratulate myself about anything, it is on just being. It is a treat to be able to appreciate simply being alive and usually that treat is not available when I am in the company of others. It tends to get lost in the crowd.

Nonetheless, I am not so sold on solitude as was Henry David Thoreau, the American philosopher who spent months on end alone on Walden Pond. He, apparently, did have deep thoughts deep in the woods. Wrote Thoreau: "I never found a companion that was so companionable as solitude."

No, I value my time with good friends too much to go that far. But Thoreau does get me thinking about an activity that lies between solitude and time spent with a truly companionable friend, and that is time spent with people when intimacy is not an option. There is a lot of that in our lives—for example, a party, the kind where people flit from group to group and shmooze amiably, often entertainingly, but not really personally. At such gatherings, it is nearly impossible to feel even an intimation of intimacy.

I prefer solitude to that. This may well be an old man thing that comes from a sense of time running out and not wanting to waste a moment of it. I would rather spend my remaining time breathing in and out in my chair behind the house than spend it being the life of a party.

I have noticed that as Snookers gets older, he tends to spend more time alone, too. Rather than go for a walk with me, he often prefers to remain lying beneath a spreading maple tree with his head held up, sniffing the passing scene, occasionally wagging his tail, perhaps in response to an intriguing smell.

Does this mean that in our old age, Snookers and I are withdrawing from the world? Letting go of the activities and encounters that once enriched our lives so that we can now pass gracefully to a world of nothingness? I don't know. But I do know that sitting alone out in the backyard my life can feel very rich indeed.

Albert Einstein expressed this late-in-life phenomenon beautifully when he wrote, "I live in that solitude which is painful in youth, but delicious in the years of maturity."

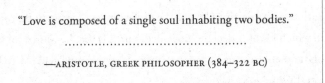

"Love is composed of a single soul inhabiting two bodies."

....

—ARISTOTLE, GREEK PHILOSOPHER (384–322 BC)

IF ARISTOTLE HAD HAD A CLUE TO HOW MANY RELATIONSHIPS HE would wreck with these ten simple words, he might have reconsidered composing them. In comparison to this version of Ideal Love, our garden-variety love affairs and marriages seem a pale shade of drab. And inevitably, along with drab comes discontent: "We just don't seem like a single soul, honey. So let's call it quits."

I was already a Soul-Mate Romantic when I copied that line from Aristotle into my notebook. We were all romantics then. As kids, we had heard Rhett Butler in *Gone with the Wind* declare to his beloved: "Scarlett! Look at me! I've loved you more than I've ever loved any woman and I've waited for you longer than I've ever waited for any woman." We totally bought into Rhett's rhetoric, especially that "waiting long" part, because clearly if there is only one perfect soul mate to a customer, we were not going to come across him or her for a very long time, if ever.

We marveled when Daisy Buchanan murmured to Gatsby: "I wish I'd done everything on earth with you," because we just knew that any experience *without* our perfect mate was merely a warm-up for the real thing. We listened repeatedly to Sinatra croon that anthem of predestined love to the perfect mate, "It Had to Be You," in which Frankie declares how fortunate it is that he waited for his one and only, the one woman who could make him "glad just to be sad thinkin' of you."

And in high school we read Byron, pretended publicly that it was corny drivel, but in private were completely captivated by the poet's depiction of profound, undying love: "Long, long shall I rue thee, Too deeply to tell."

So by the time I read Aristotle's definition of love in college, I was already a goner. And then, seeing my romantic fantasy articulated so exquisitely by this great philosopher, my fantasy felt validated.

In our era, the one-soul-in-two-bodies credo meant that each individual had his own predestined soul mate, that deep down we knew and loved this person before we even met her. Further, the search for this person might be endless. And most significantly, any lover who was not that perfect soul mate was a bad choice by definition.

The result for many of us was to go through one partner after another who didn't measure up, who wasn't the perfect soul mate, who actually had an identity/soul that was solely her own and wasn't identical to ours. It never crossed our minds that we were in love with an ideal that had very little to do with flesh and blood— especially not with flesh. Many of us were deeply disappointed when the earth failed to move, as Hemingway (in *For Whom the Bell Tolls*) had assured us it would when we made love to our true soul mate. The more analytic among us went so far as to embrace the then-popular criterion for a perfect match: simultaneous orgasms. This criterion had the advantage of being as measurable as an Aristotelian triangle; we could determine a perfect match in just a few overnight experiments, often turning lovemaking into a joyless affair.

Aristotle's formulation has its roots in a dialogue, *The Symposium*, written by his teacher, Plato, in which Socrates and some of his cronies sing praises of Eros, the god of love. One member of this seminar, Aristophanes (here as a fictional character), declares that true lovers gravitate to one another because our forefathers were androgynous beings with a face on each side of their heads, so by joining one another lovers were actually making themselves whole again. Aristotle's influence could still be seen centuries later in the work of the Roman poet Ovid, who frequently referred to love and friendship in terms of "two in body, one in mind."

It was not until I was somewhat older that I realized that Aristotle actually did have something instructive to say to modern lovers. Rereading passages about relationships in his *Nicomachean Ethics*, I began to understand that what he meant by a soul mate was a form of what he called "complete friendship" as compared to "friendships for utility" and "friendships solely for pleasure." He wrote: "[C]omplete friendship is that of good people, those who are alike in their virtue: they each alike wish good things to each other in so far as they are good." In short, suitable partners feel drawn to each other's fundamental character. "They are disposed in this way towards each other because of what they are, not for any incidental reason." And "Such friendship is, as one might expect, lasting, since in it are combined all the qualities that friends should have." Finally, coming to his concept of romantic love, Aristotle wrote, "[I]t tends to be a sort of excess of friendship, and it is felt towards a single person." There is something charming about that phrase, an "excess of friendship." It beautifully captures the idea of overflowing with good feelings.

I think one thing Aristotle is teaching here is a lesson that took me and many of my friends a long time to appreciate: For the long haul, it's a damned good idea to find a relationship in which you just naturally want to be good to each other—in fact, a relationship in which you can be good to one another *simply by being yourself.* If the catchphrase for that concept is "a single soul inhabiting two bodies," I guess I'll take it after all.

> "Nothing happens while you live. The scenery changes,
> people come in and go out, that's all. There are no
> beginnings. Days are tacked on to days without rhyme
> or reason, an interminable, monotonous addition."
>
> ....
>
> —JEAN-PAUL SARTRE, FRENCH PHILOSOPHER
> (1905–1980), EXISTENTIALIST

THIS ENTRY APPEARS ABOUT HALFWAY THROUGH MY NOTEBOOK, written with a Bic ballpoint pen as I sat in the Jardin du Luxembourg during my very brief tenure studying philosophy at the Sorbonne. I find myself both touched and embarrassed by the earnestness of my younger self in the note I scribbled below it:

I have been there, Jean-Paul. I have sung that blues of all blues, the There's-Nothing-New-Under-The-Sun Blues, the Fighting-Vainly-The-Old-Ennui Blues, the Same-Old-Same-Old-Thing Blues. The Existential Blues. . . . I have felt myself drowning in the monotony of it all. I have despaired of ever finding anything new and meaningful.

I can picture my distant young self sitting alone on a park

bench, the collar of my coat turned up, an unfiltered cigarette dangling from my lips, my eyes squinted as I took in the dreary predictability of everything I saw. I grimaced as I beheld the false bonhomie of middle-aged couples chatting. And I shuddered as I watched young lovers locked in an embrace, totally unaware that their affair would inevitably turn into mutual contempt or worse, boredom.

It was not pretty. But at those times in my life when I felt this existential ennui, it was very real. It made me wonder why I should bother to do anything, like get out of bed in the morning.

If I felt and acted that way today, someone would trot me off to a shrink where I would be promptly diagnosed with Recurrent Depressive Disorder (Code 296.32 in the *Diagnostic and Statistical Manual of Mental Disorders*) and medicated with Prozac. One thing about living in a psychological era is that few people give credence or value to a philosophical perspective. In our period, despairing of finding any meaning in life is rarely considered a sincerely held worldview; no, it is a sickness that needs to be cured. If I said to a psychiatrist that by treating existential ennui as a disease he is making the gratuitous assumption that the correct way to live is cheerfully and hopefully, he would look at me as if I was, well, sick in the head. Most shrinks presuppose that the goal of life is to become positive and to have a sense of well-being and that it is not healthy to feel or think otherwise.

But what if, after philosophical contemplation, a person finds life empty? What if he cannot find any meaning in life, either rationally or in the depths of his being? Does that simply mean it's Prozac time?

The "Nothing happens while you live" quote is from Sartre's first novel, *Nausea*. Written in 1938, it was a philosophical treatise in literary form. The story involves a man who gradually loses his grip on everything that once had meaning and value in his life; hence the "nausea" of endless meaninglessness that overcomes him. Near the end of the novel, this man begins to grasp that he alone can create the meaning of his life. This freedom is horrifying in both its arbitrariness and its personal responsibility, but it is also thrilling. The novel's theme of suffering as a prerequisite for consciousness— that "life begins on the other side of despair"—made *Nausea* an indispensable text of the Existentialist movement.

I experienced bouts of existential despair for a good part of my twenties. Looking back on that period now, I can see that some of that feeling was mixed up with my gloom over my inability to find a satisfying vocation and my failed love affairs. But even now I am not convinced that my personal problems were all there was to my despairing view of life. Indeed, my view of life had contributed to my inability to find any kind of meaningful occupation and the breakdown of my love affairs. It went both ways.

But there is another perspective on this period of my life that I only see now: at some level, I found my despair romantic. My upturned collar and dangling cigarette are dead giveaways. Very *à la mode française*. That the most compelling formulations of existential despair were French clearly contributed to this romanticism. It was not simply that French philosophers such as Sartre and Camus expressed this despair better than any other philosophers; this view of life also pervaded popular French language and art. The Nouvelle Vague films of the day portrayed antiheroes beset by a sense of meaninglessness and the inertia born of that feeling. I will never forget the almost unbearable emptiness I felt when I saw Louis Malle's film *Le Feu Follet* (*The Fire Within*) in 1963. The film records the final forty-eight hours of a failed writer who, overcome with a sense of meaninglessness, has resolved to kill himself. I saw the film twice on succeeding days and felt nauseous both times.

I also remember seeing attractive Sorbonne students in Paris cafés shrugging with soulful resignation and intoning, "*Je m'en fous,*" a fashionable phrase of the day that meant, roughly, "Not only do I not give a shit, but it wouldn't make any difference if I did." As I say, very French and very romantic. I was very young.

Yet even this personal admission does not reduce what I thought and felt in that period to something trivial. In a far less dramatic way than for the protagonists in *Nausea* or *The Fire Within*, I, too, needed to work my way through my existential despair to get a grip on my life. Fortunately, I did—well, some of the time.

———

Recently, I have heard young people using the expression, "That's a First World problem." Looking up that pop aphorism on the Web, I came across a photograph of a poverty-stricken child in South America and under it the caption, "So you're telling me you have so much clean water that you shit in it?" The implication is, of course, that the vast majority of our complaints and anxieties are over First World problems, trivialities when compared to Third World problems.

Well, these days I often think that sitting on a park bench dwelling on the meaninglessness of it all is a First World indulgence. The child in that photograph will probably never become preoccupied with the meaning of his life; he will become preoccupied with finding enough food and water to simply stay alive. But that said, I still do not begrudge myself that period of existential despair. Or, as Edith Piaf dolefully sang on the radio in those days, *"Je ne regrette rien."*

A note about Prozac: I am absolutely all for taking Prozac if that is the choice a person makes. Even if a person is beset by the existential blues, if he chooses to change the way he feels via medication, he has made a personal choice I fully respect.

I know staunch Existentialists would disagree. They say that taking a pill that not only changes your mood, but changes your entire outlook on life, is an act of "bad faith." This pill-taker is "unauthentic," because he is treating himself as an object rather than as a subject. He is acting as if his world outlook is just another "thing" to be manipulated.

Perhaps. But when I read the book *Listening to Prozac* by Dr. Peter Kramer, I was struck by how many pill-takers stated that once their depression lifted, they felt more like their "true selves" than ever before.

> "The life of man is of no greater importance to the universe than that of an oyster."
>
> ···
>
> —DAVID HUME, PHILOSOPHER
> (1711–1776), BRITISH EMPIRICIST

THIS IS ONE OF THE FIRST QUOTES I COPIED INTO MY NOTEBOOK as a young man. It spoke to me then and it speaks to me now. Indeed, the ultimate insignificance of my life in the context of the entire universe and time eternal becomes harder to ignore as I near its end. But these days I find a sweet consolation just beneath the surface of Hume's assessment.

For starters, I need to check out a bit of ambiguity in Hume's statement. Does he mean that all lives—from oyster to human—are of equal importance to the universe, yet they are all of *great* importance to it? That every little thing is absolutely wonderful in God's handmade universe, like the "It's all good" message of the Anglican hymn, "All Things Bright and Beautiful"?

I'm afraid not. It would be unlike Hume, a skeptical philosopher, to be in such a warm and fuzzy frame of mind when he issued his oyster ordinance. Rather, I suspect he meant something along the lines of, "It is all so incredibly big out there and each one of us is so incredibly small, our lives so brief and time infinitely long, so maybe our individual lives are not the big deals we like to think they are. In fact, our lives are more like an oyster's."

At first blush, this is definitely not a feel-good memo. It implies that our individual lives are so puny against the backdrop of the cosmos as to be utterly meaningless. What is more, Hume has us coming and going: If the cosmos is operating according to some grand plan, we are simply tiny cogs in the Humongous Machine; but if all is random in the cosmos, our lives are also random, plus shrimpy on top of that.

I will never forget the time my wife, Freke, and I spent a few days in Corfu on our way from Italy to mainland Greece. Freke has always had a fondness for viewing out-of-the-way historical sites and this time she wanted to see the tomb of a ninth-century AD potentate who had once ruled all of Asia Minor. We took a public bus to somewhere deep in the island's interior where the driver let us off beside a copse of ancient olive trees, pointing toward a long, rocky road. We trekked for almost an hour and then we finally saw it: a small, toppling cairn bearing a sign in Greek and English with the name of this man who had once been emperor of what was then a sizeable chunk of the civilized world. There were a couple of bottles of Hillas beer lying beside it. That was it. So much for immortality via memorabilia. I found the ultimate smallness of the great king's life both sad and wryly comical, but mostly deeply humbling.

This little tableau immediately reminded me of Percy Bysshe Shelley's poignant sonnet "Ozymandias," written upon seeing a statue in the Egyptian desert of the once-powerful Rameses II. Here are the poem's last six lines:

> *And on the pedestal these words appear:*
> *"My name is Ozymandias, king of kings:*
> *Look on my works, ye Mighty, and despair!"*
> *Nothing beside remains: round the decay*
> *Of that colossal wreck, boundless and bare,*
> *The lone and level sands stretch far away.*

But there is another way of looking at the oyster enigma, and that is from the point of view of the American pop philosophical school known as the It's a Wonderful Life theorists. (Okay, there isn't really a legitimate philosophical school by this name, but that doesn't stop me from considering it.) According to this thesis, our tiny lives can have a colossal ripple effect. Witness the difference it would have made to the people of Bedford Falls if George Bailey had never lived, as demonstrated by Clarence Odbody, Angel Second Class. For those who somehow missed this movie, *It's a Wonderful Life* is a classic Frank Capra film about a man, George Bailey, who contemplates suicide because he thinks he has failed his family and community, but Angel Clarence sets George straight by showing him how Bedford Falls would have turned out if

George had never existed. Not good at all, and that is because George significantly affected the lives around him with his small acts of kindness. The idea is that every little thing we do has repercussions that reach far and wide even if we do appear oysterlike.

The Wonderful Life theory is a social-behavior variation on the Butterfly Effect, which suggests that the flap of a butterfly's wings in one part of the globe can be the determining cause of a hurricane in another part of the globe. Devised by Edward Lorenz, an American meteorologist and chaos theory physicist, the Butterfly Effect basically postulates that over time a small event can generate big changes. So be it for George Bailey's small acts of kindness, not to mention yours and mine. Of course, the problem with any chain of cause and effect is where it all begins. Like, why should the Lorenz chain start with the flapping of that butterfly's wings? Wasn't there a cause of that? And of the cause of that cause? Is it causes all the way down? But let us not go down that caterpillar hole just now.

Film culture also offers a more nuanced response to Hume's insignificant-lives paradigm. The Swedish masterpiece *Fanny and Alexander* suggests that we can take great comfort in acknowledging how small and unimportant our individual lives are because each little life can be seen as a cosmos unto itself. We are all meaningful players in the Little World.

Ingmar Bergman's deeply moving film recounts three years in the lives of an extended, wealthy Swedish family, the Ekdahls, in the early 1900s. During the course of the drama, the Ekdahls suffer some great losses—the premature death of young Alexander's father and the remarriage of his mother, Emilie, to a clergyman who turns out to be an extremely controlling husband and a cruel stepfather. Near the end, Emilie and the children are rescued and returned to the family home where they celebrate with a grand dinner. Alexander's uncle, Gustav, offers a long, sometimes humorous, and altogether loving toast that concludes with the passage below, an ode to the "little world":

"The world is a den of thieves, and night is falling. Evil breaks its chains and runs through the world like a mad dog. The poison affects us all. No one escapes. Therefore let us be happy while we are happy. Let us be kind, generous, affectionate, and good. It is necessary and not at all shameful to take pleasure in the little world."

In short, the little world is his oyster. Sounds good to me.

> "First and foremost, nothing exists; second, even if
> it exists, it is inapprehensible to man; third, even if it is
> apprehensible, still it is without doubt incapable of
> being expressed or explained to the next man."
>
> ....
>
> —GORGIAS OF LEONTINI, GREEK ORATOR AND PHILOSOPHER
> (485–380 BC), SOPHIST AND PROTO-NIHILIST
>
> ....
>
> (*As paraphrased by* SEXTUS EMPIRICUS, [160–210 AD],
> *from Gorgias's* ON THE NON-EXISTENT, *a now-lost manuscript*)

I REMEMBER EXACTLY WHY I COPIED THIS ONE INTO MY NOTEBOOK in my midtwenties: to remind myself just how wacky all that meaningless-of-it-all philosophy can seem sometimes. Old Gorgias turned nihilistic doctrine into deadpan drollery.

The construction of Gorgias's above argument still cracks me up. It sounds like an old eastern European insult joke: "You aren't my brother, but even if you were my brother, I would have nothing to do with you, and even if I had something to do with you, it wouldn't be brotherly."

Gorgias, an orator famous for his parodies, was ancient Greece's equivalent of a hip stand-up comedian. I guess if it is delivered with an ironic smile, the statement "Nothing exists" can be a real thigh-slapper. Gorgias knocked 'em dead from Delphi to Olympia, charging admission for his performances and making himself a very nice living. One problem translators and scholars have with his opus is that they can never be sure whether he really meant what he wrote or he was just spoofing.

Gorgias's enterprise of wringing laughs out of an abject assessment of life raises some fascinating questions about humor—how it can help us cope and how it sometimes does just the opposite. Psychologists believe that humor is a creative defense mechanism for distancing ourselves from anxious-making thoughts and feelings. Sex makes us anxious, particularly adulterous sex, so there are legions of sex and infidelity gags in virtually every culture. And, of course, consciousness of mortality—particularly our own—induces the ultimate angst, so again, gags galore. But sometimes these gags fall flat; or worse, they make the pain *less* bearable.

After 9/11, the accepted wisdom was that irony was dead and that certainly that particular horror would never become a joking matter. Then, only three weeks after the event, the comedian Gilbert Gottfried opened his routine at the Friars Club by saying, "I have a flight to California. I can't get a direct flight—they said they have to stop at the Empire State Building first."

Gottfried was loudly booed and several of his fellow comedians walked out of the hall. "Too soon," they cried. "Way too soon."

I think they were right: We needed the distance of more time before we could find even cold comfort in a 9/11 joke. Instead, Gottfried's gag just made us feel sullied, made us feel unfeeling.

Several years ago, Tom and I wrote a book about the philosophy of mortality in which we used death jokes to illustrate various philosophers' points of view. A reporter asked us if we thought joking about death really worked, if we believed it actually eased the terror of confronting our mortality. Good question. All I could answer was, "Only when it works."

I guess the same could be said for Gorgias's wisecracks about the meaningless of life.

In any event, Gorgias's arguments for the nonexistence of everything—from the physical world itself to the so-called values of society (if society existed, of course)—were straight from his cynical heart. He is one of the first recorded nihilists in Western philosophy, beginning a long tradition of philosophers who trashed everything, particularly that absurd notion that life has any meaning. Like for starters, if nothing really exists, what could there be that had meaning?

Even though Gorgias apparently led a pleasurable life, he would have none of hedonism as a philosophy, at least in his recorded teachings. I suppose that even if one is a nihilist, one could still *practice* hedonism; a life of pleasure does not necessarily need to bear any philosophical meaning, it can just *be*.

I will refrain from an *ad hominem* critique of the Greek philo-gagster based on the fact that he enjoyed an extraordinarily long and fortunate life, making pocketfuls of *dekadrachm* as he traveled from city to city wowing audiences. But I do have to laugh at Gorgias's final one-liner: At the age of 104, he told his friend Athenaeus that he attributed his longevity to the fact that "I never did anything just for the pleasure."

Ba-dum ching!

> "Estragon: We always find something, eh Didi,
>
> to give us the impression we exist?
>
> "Vladimir: Yes, yes, we're magicians."

···

—SAMUEL BECKETT, IRISH NOVELIST AND PLAYWRIGHT

(1906–1989), ABSURDIST

AH, THE BITTERSWEETNESS OF THE COSMIC JOKE. IT GETS ME every time. Gorgias definitely started a trend with his nihilistic repartee. And no one delivers this bittersweet humor with more poignancy and wit than Samuel Beckett, particularly in his classic drama *Waiting for Godot*. That play, a juggle of sincerity and irony, hope and despair, is nihilistic vaudeville, the epitome of Theater of the Absurd. Listening to Estragon and Vladimir's hilarious patter, we laugh deliciously—right up until our hearts sink at the inescapable meaninglessness of the characters' lives and, ultimately, of our own. And then we laugh again, although not so merrily this time.

I didn't see *Waiting for Godot* until well after I first put away my "Pithies" notebook, but the play affected me so strongly that I immediately purchased the playscript and read it, later copying the above lines into my reopened notebook. In addition to the drama's scathing yet comical perspective on the universal human condition, it affected me in a personal way. It summoned up a sweet and wry old memory.

When my friend Tom and I were college students, we would occasionally sit on the stone steps of his dormitory late at night and spontaneously launch into fanciful improvisations. I can't remember how this game of ours got started, but I do know that we were never intoxicated, just very tired and youthfully whimsical. I suppose our routine could be seen as some sort of ad-lib therapy: In those days both Tom and I were extremely anxious about how we would fare once we hit the adult world, and this game was a way of playing with our anxieties. At that time Tom was planning to go to divinity school, yet wasn't convinced he was cut out to be a minister; I had no plans at all.

Sitting on those steps during winter exam week of our junior year, we suddenly began reciting imaginary Christmas letters that we would exchange in the future.

"Dear Danny," Tom began, "Now that we are settled in our house and have met all the members of my new congregation, I am finally feeling that this is going to work out. . . . Incidentally, is it true that you have gone into the toy business? I heard on the grapevine that you had invented some kind of game you can play in your sleep."

"Dear Tommy, Not only am I in the toy business, but I am now living next door to my very own paddle ball factory in New Jersey. Of course, Dad is proud as all get-out. I keep telling myself this is only a step to something more exciting, but what? Beach balls? Anyway, thanks for sending along your sermon about Hope in last year's letter. It was inspiring, although I keep thinking Hope needs an object to be complete—like hoping for a sports car or a trip to Hawaii or a personal visit from God. But just plain Hope? Can't say I know that animal."

On and on we went with these made-up Christmas letters, traveling through our future years, complete with marriages, children, new jobs, and homes, our imagined lives becoming increasingly ordinary as our desire for excitement dribbled away. And then Tom began what turned out to be the last letter in our little improv, "Dear Danny, Things are quiet around the parsonage since our Tom passed away."

At that point we both began to weep. I don't think it was simply the idea of Tom dying in the distant future that caused our tears, nor even our exam-period exhaustion, although that surely contributed to it. It was our sense of meaninglessness about our coming lives—a shared and deeply felt "Is that all there is?" But there was also something comical about our little game—something absurdist. Sitting there on those stone steps we were satirizing ourselves and our predicament. For a few minutes in the winter of 1959, we were our own Estragon and Vladimir.

Novels and plays express Absurdism more tellingly than any philosophical essay can hope to do. Only through individual human voices can a writer adequately convey the experience of confronting the meaninglessness of life and then groaning in despair at the impossibility of coming to terms with this meaninglessness. Absurdism is not merely an idea about the way things are, it is the way in which that idea smacks against our lives. Samuel Beckett conveys this stunningly.

Not to be disrespectful, but consider how Søren Kierkegaard, the nineteenth-century godfather of Absurdism, addressed this phenomenon: "What is the Absurd? It is, as may quite easily be seen, that I, a rational being, must act in a case where my reason, my powers of reflection, tell me: you can just as well do the one thing as the other, that is to say where my reason and reflection say: you cannot act and yet here is where I have to act."

I grasp his point—I just don't *feel* it. Of course, the Danish philosopher was laying the groundwork for his leap from the absurd to faith in God, not a leap to despairing laughter over the meaninglessness of it all. Nonetheless, Kierkegaard makes me long for Estragon and Vladimir.

Albert Camus was the first modern philosopher to proclaim our confrontation with absurdity as a central problem of philosophy. In his seminal essay *The Myth of Sisyphus*, he wrote that Absurdism emanates from the dissonance between man's natural desire to find meaning in his life and the impossibility of finding that meaning in any rational way. The absurdity does not lie in a logical contradiction, but in an *existential* contradiction; it is the primary puzzle of human existence. We long for meaning but we can't get it.

Camus said there are three basic responses to confronting this absurdity: 1) commit suicide (life is meaningless and futile, so who needs it?); 2) take a Kierkegaardian leap of faith to a belief in God (it is just as irrational as anything else, so why not go for something really Big?); or 3) accept the absurdity of it all but carry on anyhow.

This last was the option Camus chose. It afforded a man the radical freedom to create his own meaning, to create his own life from scratch. This definitely sounds existentially thrilling, but despite the tragicomic irony of Sisyphus's endlessly repetitive and pointless task, I am not experiencing even a wee existential chuckle here.

In both French and English, the word "absurd" denotes a state of affairs that is "ludicrously incongruent." It is definitely a fitting term for this philosophy: What could be more incongruent than our need for meaning and the impossibility of finding it? But what about that "ludicrous" part? It seems to have gone missing in Camus's essay. Enter Samuel Beckett. In *Waiting for Godot*, the Cosmic Joke is center stage.

Most humor theorists put incongruity at the heart of any good gag. What's funny about a clown wearing oversized shoes? That his shoes are nothing like *normal* shoes: They are incongruent. Ditto for a platypus walking into a bar; platypi don't barhop. I sometimes think that the most practical way studying philosophy paid off for me was in how it prepared me to write gags for comedians: Philosophy is loaded with those wild incongruities known as paradoxes.

Some of my favorite old jokes are absurd to the core, like this one about Sasha in the St. Petersburg railway station:

> *Sasha goes up to another man and says, "Don't I know you?"*
>
> *The other man says, "No. We've never met."*
>
> *"Just a minute," Sasha says. "Have you ever been to Minsk?"*
>
> *"No," the other man says.*
>
> *"Neither have I," says Sasha. "Must have been two other fellows."*

But the ultimate absurdist gag is the one about the human being looking for life's meaning when there isn't any to be found. It took Beckett to wring a laugh out of that one.

> *Estragon: We always find something, eh Didi, to give us the impression we exist?*
>
> *Vladimir: Yes, yes, we're magicians.*

Ha!
Aargh!
Gasp!
Ha!

> "The philosopher who finds no meaning for this world is not
> concerned exclusively with the problem of pure metaphysics;
> he is also concerned to prove that there is no valid reason
> why he personally should not do as he wants to. . . .
> For myself . . . the philosophy of meaninglessness was
> essentially an instrument of liberation, sexual and political."
>
> ....
>
> —ALDOUS HUXLEY, BRITISH NOVELIST AND PHILOSOPHER
> (1894–1963), SOCIAL CRITIC, HUMANIST, AND SPIRITUALIST

THIS TAKE ON NIHILISM IS A HOOT, TOO, ALTHOUGH I'M SURE
humor was not Huxley's intention. He says that after all is said and
done, meaninglessness is a door that opens onto an erotic bedroom.
No emptiness, no ennui, not even a grim laugh over the absurdity
of it all—just a joyful, emancipated making of whoopee. I have to
say, meaninglessness is starting to look a lot better down here
between the sheets. Indeed, I see that I recorded this quote when I
was in my early thirties, undoubtedly as a confirmation of the life
I was somewhat guiltily leading at the time. I clearly needed an
endorsement of the idea that there was no valid reason why I, personally, should not do anything I wanted to do.

Existentialists would argue that Huxley's idea of meaning-lessness is more local than cosmic, that he is talking about the meaninglessness of the political and religious setup of society, not about the big picture of the Meaninglessness of It All. They are right: Huxley is implicitly confirming that a liberated roll in the hay does have terrific value, so not *all* can be meaningless.

Meaninglessness in philosophical nihilism covers a wide spectrum, ranging from Metaphysical Nihilism, a negation of all existence, to Moral and Political Nihilism, a negation of a society's values and laws in a world that we acknowledge exists but has the potential to be better. In this last sense, it is easy to see how breaking away from the inherited truths of society, governments, and religion can make life more enjoyable in an old-fashioned, hedonistic sort of way.

Aldous Huxley possessed a preternatural talent for spotting the coming zeitgeist a mile away. When he wrote his classic novel *Brave New World* in 1932, he foresaw medical human reproductive tech-niques that became common practice half a century later; more significantly, he anticipated brainwashing methods that later would be used to control and dehumanize entire populations. And in the early 1950s, when he took his first dose of mescaline, the hal-lucinogen derived from the peyote cactus, and wrote about his extraordinary experiences in *The Doors of Perception*, he placed himself in the vanguard of the psychedelic mania that arrived over a decade later. Between the advent of the contraceptive pill and the radical perspective that came from mind-altering drugs, Huxley not only anticipated the liberated consciousness of the 1960s, he was a major player in its creation. It was that consciousness that gave birth to the Sexual Revolution. Annulling the strictures of church and state, newly liberated folks decided that sex need not entail either sin or guilt. Lust was just plain fun, so go for it.

And go for it we did in that era, right up until some of us started to sense that sex as simply a pleasurable sport did have some drawbacks. Hearts still got broken. Mutual trust became more complicated. "Open marriages" didn't last. And a sense of isolation and loneliness descended on some of us as the concept of love became more elusive than ever. Much to our disappointment, sexual liberation turned out to come with a price tag. Even the great prophet Huxley had not forecast that.

In Huxley's case, sexual freedom presented a problem that may be peculiar to hard-driven writers: Sex squandered too much of his time. In one biography of Huxley, the author notes that Huxley's first wife, Maria, encouraged her husband to have affairs: "Maria thought that he enjoyed such distractions, needed the change and his mind taken off his work." But in the end, Maria needed to select the candidates for these affairs and work out their logistics because "Aldous was disinclined to waste time on the intricacies of courtship." In any event, these assignations appeared to be little more than trifling distractions for him, so eager was he to get back to his desk. That does not exactly sound like revolutionary liberation, but I guess it's the thought that counts.

> "There's a great difficulty in making choices if you have any imagination at all. Faced with such a multitude of desirable choices, no one choice seems satisfactory for very long by comparison with the aggregate desirability of all the rest, though compared to any 'one' of the others it would not be found inferior."
>
> ....
>
> —JOHN BARTH, AMERICAN NOVELIST
> (1930–), EXISTENTIALIST

DELIGHTFULLY, SOME GIFTED AMERICAN FICTION WRITERS PICKED up Absurdist witcraft where the French Existentialists left off. When I first read John Barth's *The End of the Road* in the early 1960s, I laughed myself silly. Here was a quintessentially American take on Continental Existentialism. As with the central character in Sartre's *Nausea*, the first-person protagonist of Barth's novel, Jake Horner, suffers from the meaninglessness-of-it-all blues, but Horner is seriously neurotic on top of that—*farcically* neurotic. His poker-faced reflections on the impossibility of making ordinary choices is high comedy, more Woody Allen befuddlement than Samuel Beckett absurdism.

Yes, Barth says, we have this terrifying privilege of creating our own meaning of life, but for starters, how the hell do we make all the little decisions that actually make up our daily lives?

Just recalling the first scene of *The End of the Road* makes me smile. Horner goes up to the ticket window in the Baltimore railway station and asks where he can go for thirty dollars. Told that his options are Cincinnati, Crestline, Dayton, or Lima, Ohio, he withdraws to a bench in the waiting room where he realizes that there is no compelling reason for him to go anywhere, including back to his apartment, so he simply stays there. Horner says, "I simply ran out of motives, as a car runs out of gas. There was no reason to do anything. My eyes were fixed on ultimacy, and when that is the case there is no reason to do anything—even to change the focus of one's eyes."

Next day, still paralyzed on his railway station bench, Horner is approached by a doctor who diagnoses him with "cosmopsis"— a Barth neologism for the inability to choose from all imaginable choices. So off Horner goes to the doctor's clinic, Remobilization Farm, for therapy that includes reading both the works of Sartre and the *World Almanac*. Until Horner gets a hold on his life, the doctor prescribes a method for making his daily choices: "[D]on't let yourself get stuck between alternatives, or you're lost. You're not that strong. If the alternatives are side by side, choose the one on the left; if they're consecutive in time, choose the earlier. If neither of these applies, choose the alternative whose name begins with the earlier letter of the alphabet. These are the principles of Sinistrality,

Antecedence, and Alphabetical Priority—there are others, and they're arbitrary, but useful."

The doctor's treatment for overcoming choice-making paralysis then goes on to "mythotherapy," adopting "masks" to abolish the ego by acting out symbolic roles. This is Existentialism gone wacky.

Beside its comedy, the main reason *The End of the Road* means so much to me is that it brings Existentialism directly into ordinary life, where Existentialism properly belongs. No hard-to-fathom abstractions about Being and Nothingness here. This is an uproarious manual on how to get through a day when every alternative seems equally worthless. Hilariously, it calls on good old-fashioned American know-how to solve the problem of meaninglessness.

In the quote I copied out from *The End of the Road*, Barth/Horner lays out a particular problem facing the choice-maker, one that ups the ante of my old friend Habib's predicament of choosing between individual options. Horner's predicament is that *all* the available options out there seem a whole lot better than any particular single option does. This is because he makes a dumb mistake: He weighs *all* of those options against just *one* of the options. Why even bring up such a stupid miscalculation?

Because that is the way even the smartest people experience their options. This dumb mistake is built into our make-up. Dumb or not, we want *all* the possibilities that there are and it is a real downer that we only get to choose one—or at least just one at a time. It is enough to give a person the existential blues.

———

There is another American existentialist novel from the 1960s that makes the problems of choice-making and self-creation come alive for me in a way that no European philosopher had. That is Walker Percy's stunning *The Moviegoer*. It is about a fellow with the musical name of Binx Bolling whose life is so empty that he is always either daydreaming or getting totally involved in the lives of characters in movies, radio programs, and books. But then he has a breakthrough of consciousness and sets out on a quest for meaning. Says Binx, "What is the nature of the search? you ask. Really it is very simple; at least for a fellow like me. So simple that it is easily overlooked. The search is what anyone would undertake if he were not sunk in the everydayness of his own life."

"Everydayness" is a key concept in Existentialism. It describes the way we get so immersed in the routines and roles of our daily lives that we never experience full consciousness of who we are and what choices are available to us. The German Existentialist Martin Heidegger wrote about it extensively in his magnum opus *Being and Time*. I once tried to read a chapter in that tome about "everydayness": It said something about the concept of *das Man*, "the person who is above all the space of existence in which it is impossible to find individuality." I did not find this description very illuminating. Maybe it was the translation.

The Existentialist psychologist Viktor Frankl put it more lucidly when he coined the term "Sunday neurosis," defining it as "that kind of depression which afflicts people who become aware of the lack of content in their lives when the rush of the busy week is over and the void within themselves becomes manifest."

Binx Bolling helps me understand "everydayness" in the gut. And both Barth and Percy helped me realize once again that some philosophical ideas—especially those about how best to live—can be most meaningfully conveyed through fiction.

> "In the golden rule of Jesus of Nazareth, we read the complete spirit of the ethics of utility. 'To do as you would be done by,' and 'to love your neighbor as yourself,' constitute the ideal perfection of utilitarian morality."
>
> ....
>
> —JOHN STUART MILL, ENGLISH PHILOSOPHER
> (1806–1873), UTILITARIAN

I OFTEN FIND MYSELF COMING BACK TO THAT AFFECTING CODA TO *Fanny and Alexander*: "The world is a den of thieves, and night is falling. Evil breaks its chains and runs through the world like a mad dog. The poison affects us all. No one escapes. Therefore let us be happy while we are happy. Let us be kind, generous, affectionate, and good. It is necessary and not at all shameful to take pleasure in the little world."

But increasingly that phrase, "not at all shameful," troubles me. Like many people I know, I sometimes feel guilty for living in a fortunate bubble, one where too often I am oblivious to the evil running like a mad dog through the bigger world. Being a hedonist with a conscience can be demoralizing. It turns out that this business of feeling good often comes at the price of somebody else's deprivation, and then I have to consider which is more important to me: *feeling* good or *being* good? Reading Mill has always been instructive for me on this dilemma, starting when I read the quoted line as a student.

I have always liked the Golden Rule, in part because it is so pithy. It makes its point fast and then lets you work out the details as situations present themselves. Very tidy. No wonder that virtually every culture has come up with a maxim that is practically identical to it.

But the Golden Rule of the Bible asks me to accept it as a matter of faith. It is the basic way to be good and therefore to make God happy with me. So, if I have a tenuous grasp on divine faith, I am left wondering, why? Why be good to others? To put it callously, what's in it for me?

Mill has the answer: The Golden Rule is a utilitarian concept. It is in my own best interest to follow the Golden Rule because by following it I will promote the greatest good for the greatest number of people, and that, most of the time, is good for *me*. So what we have here is virtuous behavior as enlightened self-interest.

But I am still left with the question, how does my following the Golden Rule ensure that the people around me will follow it also? I guess it's a deal we make with the rest of society: I will follow the Golden Rule if you do, and that way we'll all get along just fine.

But you go first, okay?

It's in that "you go first" business that things can get messy. It opens up what moral philosophers call the "free-rider problem," in which all it takes to screw up a Golden Rule–abiding society is for a few people to cheat by taking a free ride on everybody else's goodwill.

One of the few times I ever got angry at my friend Johanna was over just such a "free-ride" issue. As a devoted follower of Anthroposophy—Rudolf Steiner's early-twentieth-century spiritual philosophy that comes with comprehensive rules of conduct—Johanna did not believe in inoculating her children against whooping cough. Steiner had declared that "these inoculations will influence the human body in a way that will make it refuse to give a home to the spiritual inclinations of the soul." So Johanna did not vaccinate her children.

But the ultimate way inoculations do their job is by ridding an *entire population* of a deadly disease. For example, the Salk-Sabin vaccine against polio has virtually eradicated that disease in most of the Western world, so much so that children here who have not gotten the vaccine run virtually no risk of getting the disease. Through vaccines, whooping cough has *almost* been eradicated, but not quite— here and there the germ is still alive and can be transmitted from child to child. So Johanna's children, without their inoculations, now run very little risk of getting whooping cough, but they are getting a free ride on the rest of the children who do get the inoculations. And on the unlikely yet increased chance that her children do get whooping cough, they are putting other children at risk, say, very young children who have not yet been inoculated. Not fair, I said to Johanna.

Why should her children get a free ride on all the children who *do* get inoculations? If she believes that the benefit to her kids is that it will give a home to their spiritual inclinations, does that mean that she thinks they are more deserving of a spiritual life than all the other kids? Somehow I don't think that she would skip giving her kids the whooping cough vaccine if their likelihood of getting the disease was what it was before the vaccine was introduced to our society as a whole. Then, it was a significant cause of infant deaths.

Ultimately, if a sufficient number of people take a free ride on the Golden Rule pact, the system fails. In this case, whooping cough will stage a comeback and everyone will suffer. Nope, a free ride is not fair. It's a breach of our Golden Rule deal.

> "I don't think there's much point in bemoaning the state of the world unless there's some way you can think of to improve it. Otherwise, don't bother writing a book; go and find a tropical island and lie in the sun."
>
> ....
>
> —PETER SINGER, AUSTRALIAN-AMERICAN PHILOSOPHER
> (1946–), MORAL PHILOSOPHER

I ONLY HEARD ABOUT SINGER A FEW YEARS AGO WHEN HE STARTED making headlines with his strict pronouncements on the ethical treatment of animals. Reading up on him, I discovered that he also had a lot to say about the ethical treatment of humans, one of my favorite species. What I immediately liked about this philosopher is that he takes moral philosophy out of the general and abstract and puts it smack in front of us as concrete ethical dilemmas.

What I don't like about Peter Singer is that after reading him I often feel guilty. *Very* guilty.

These two are closely related: I end up feeling guilty because usually I don't actually *do* the things that his concrete moral scenarios convince me that I should do.

Here is an example of the way Singer gets to us: He recounts the plot of the Brazilian film *Central Station*, in which a poor woman, Dora, suddenly has the chance to make a quick thousand dollars. All she has to do is persuade a little street urchin to go with her to a house where, she has been told, wealthy foreigners want to adopt him. Dora does the job and then uses her newly acquired money to buy herself a color TV. But then someone informs her that the boy is not really going to be adopted; his vital organs are going to be surgically harvested and sold on the black market, leaving the organless boy to die.

At this point, everyone who hears this story is horrified. We have not a single doubt that it is morally incumbent upon Dora to try to rectify the horror she has unknowingly aided. No one in his right moral mind would say, Hey, it's just another poor street kid and Dora sure is enjoying her new television set, so what the hell. That would be unconscionable. (In the film, Dora does the right thing.)

This is when Singer closes in for the kill: He informs us that in the First World we spend over a third of our money on nonessentials like color TVs. Instead, we could take that money and give it to Oxfam to aid the street urchins of Rio—to feed them and keep them safe from harm. Singer says that ultimately there is no difference between Dora's choices and our own. The exact same moral principle is involved in both cases. So we should do what we all have agreed is the morally right thing.

It is hard to refute Singer's argument, although that has not stopped many from trying. Most of these counterarguments are practical rather than moral: *How can we be certain that Oxfam will do its job fairly and properly? Doesn't charity ultimately lead to dependence and laziness?* Those kinds of rationales don't get much traction with me.

The more nuanced, philosophical counterarguments point out that Singer is working by analogy—Dora's action or inaction about the boy is analogous to our action or inaction on giving to Oxfam. But Singer's analogy is imperfect. For example, if we decide not to give to Oxfam we are *not actively* contributing to anybody's death, whereas by bringing the boy to those foreigners, Dora was *actively*, even if unwittingly, contributing to his death.

True. In fact, strictly speaking, no analogies are perfect. If they were, they wouldn't be analogies, they would be equivalents. In any event, this "actively" versus "nonactively" argument does not cut it for me either. Once we know the probable outcomes of our actions, that distinction does not strike me as significant. So basically I buy Singer's analogy and his argument.

Nonetheless, although I do have a fair number of nonessential items around the house, I admit that I don't give a dime to Oxfam. I suppose that means that I am essentially an immoral person. I cannot say I feel very good about that; in fact, sometimes when I think about it, I feel awful. I definitely need to think more about this. Or maybe I just need to *do* something, like tithe up to Oxfam already.

Yet somehow my moral inaction does not prevent me from

agreeing wholeheartedly with Singer's snipe against people who moan and groan about all the injustices of the world while never getting out of their comfy chairs to actually do something about those injustices. Call me a hypocrite. In fact, call me the most devious kind of hypocrite—one who is hypocritical about what he calls hypocrisy. But I cannot abide these moaners and groaners who believe that by earnestly and loudly voicing their moral judgments, they will make a particle of difference in the world. They make me want to actively pour a bucket of Third World water over their First World heads.

> "A man who strives after goodness in all
> his acts is sure to come to ruin, since there are
> so many men who are not good."
>
> ....
>
> —NICCOLÒ MACHIAVELLI, ITALIAN PHILOSOPHER AND DIPLOMAT
> (1469–1527), POLITICAL PHILOSOPHER

WHEN I AM FEELING BAD ABOUT NOT BEING GOOD—LIKE AFTER reading one of Peter Singer's moral dilemma fables—it is always invigorating to take a deep swig of Machiavelli, the Ethicist of Bad.

In his famous essay *The Prince*, Machiavelli laid out a detailed program for how to get ahead in the world. The Florentine philosopher may have been the first to write what Amazon.com now calls "A Life Motivation and Self-Help Book." God knows, when I copied this line into my notebook back in the 1960s, I needed all the motivation and help I could get.

The Prince's underlying principle is that "might is right." What we *ought* to do is get the job done; so what we *should* do is whatever it takes to get that job done, even if that involves deceit and fraud. Forget about "doing good" as our principal "ought"; it just muddies things up. There are wars to be won, nations to be annexed, people to be subjugated so they will not become unruly.

Not only is "doing good" a waste of time and resources, it is counterproductive: It gives our competitors just the advantage they need to screw us. Because we can count on it: They are not dithering about what is the "right thing to do" as they reach for their daggers.

The Church, of course, did not approve of Machiavelli's thesis. Since its inception, the Church has been of the Goodness-Is-Its-Own-Reward school of ethics. One does not do the right thing for personal gain; one does it simply to be a good person. Well, that and to please God, but ultimately these two are pretty much the same. What is more, if doing good requires a personal sacrifice, it puts a person up into an even higher level of goodness.

Long before the Church weighed in on levels of goodness, this hierarchy had already been elaborated by the Hebrews in the ancient text of rules and laws, the Talmud. Interpreting the Talmud, the medieval scholar Maimonides laid out the levels of *Tzedakah* (charity), from lowest to highest:

1. Giving begrudgingly.
2. Giving less than you should, but giving it cheerfully.
3. Giving after being asked.
4. Giving before being asked.
5. Giving when you do not know the recipient's identity, but the recipient knows your identity.
6. Giving when you know the recipient's identity, but the recipient does not know your identity.

7. Giving when neither party knows the other's identity.

8. Enabling the recipient to become self-reliant.

You've got to love the subtle distinctions between these levels. That last one always catches me by surprise; it is the moral rationale behind state-sponsored welfare in modern civilization.

In answer to the fundamental question of why to even participate in charity in the first place, Maimonides deconstructs the word *Tzedakah*. Its roots are righteousness, justice, and fairness, so rather than being an act of generosity, providing for the poor is a performance of *duty*, of giving the needy their due. But why should we do our duty? Well, here we go again, back into the realm of self-interest: In the Talmudic tradition doing the right thing is usually a way to encourage God to forgive a sin or even to grant a special favor, as in "I gave a mule to that destitute farmer, Itzak, now would You *please* find a husband for my eldest daughter already?"

Many philosophers have elaborated on the Goodness-Is-Its-Own-Reward idea. An avowed anti-Catholic, Maurice Maeterlinck, the twentieth-century Belgian philosopher and playwright, weighed in with: "An act of goodness is of itself an act of happiness. No reward coming after the event can compare with the sweet reward that went with it."

This is not quite the same thing as saying that goodness is its own reward. Maeterlinck adds a special quality to that reward: It makes the do-gooder feel happy. In a sense, this is Moral Hedonism—doing the right thing for the pleasure of it. So in the end, Maeterlinck's principle does not feel significantly more "ethical" to me than Machiavelli's—both principles are based on self-interest.

Perhaps both philosophers were simply trying to tell it like it is: People rarely do the good thing unless there is something in it for them. We just need to face that. Way back at the beginning of the Common Era, the Roman poet Ovid summed up the entire "doing good/reward" calculus simply, if cynically: "Men do not value a good deed unless it brings a reward."

It is hard to take Machiavellianism seriously as a moral philosophy because there is nothing moral about it. But maybe that is the point: In the end, maybe moral philosophy, with its abstract arguments about the principles of right and wrong, is not really that relevant to our lives. When the German twentieth-century playwright Bertolt Brecht was asked what he thought of ethics, he replied, "First grub, then ethics." He was implying that ethical decision-making may only be a luxury reserved for those of us who do not need to struggle simply to stay alive.

> "[O]ur moral heart strings . . . were designed to be tugged, but not from very far away. But it's not because it's [morally] good for us to be that way. It's because caring about ourselves and our small little tribal group helped us survive, and caring about the other groups—the competition—didn't help us survive. If anything, we should have negative attitudes towards them. We're competing with them for resources."

....

—JOSHUA GREENE, AMERICAN PSYCHOLOGIST AND PHILOSOPHER
(1976–), BEHAVIORAL PSYCHOLOGIST AND MORAL PHILOSOPHER

PROFESSOR GREENE IS A MORAL PHILOSOPHER WHOM EVEN Bertolt Brecht could like. He is that rare ethicist who wants to take a good look at how we actually *do* behave before he offers any prescriptions for how we *ought* to behave. He wants to make moral philosophy relevant and useful. Good idea.

It was not that long ago that psychology was considered a branch of philosophy. Both are concerned with understanding the workings of the human mind, so it made perfect sense. But in the late nineteenth century, psychology became a subject unto itself, associating itself with science and the scientific method. It was determined that the human psyche and human behavior could be measured and codified like other objects of scientific scrutiny. Theories of personality were developed; the unconscious was "discovered"; irrational behavior was explained.

Many philosophers, particularly philosophers of science, were skeptical. For example, what, exactly, could the unconscious—an object that cannot be seen or touched—possibly be? And then the philosopher Karl Popper asserted that the Oedipus complex failed the test of falsifiability, that is, there is no conceivable evidence that could prove the oedipal theory wrong, so it is worthless. Many philosophers accused psychology of scientism—employing scientific methods to study phenomena that are inherently unavailable to scientific study.

Most relevantly here, moral philosophers took exception to the way some psychologists conflated the way people *do* behave with the way people *ought* to behave. These philosophers point to the fallacious "appeal to nature"—the assumption that what is natural is inherently good. And it is not only psychologists who make this mistake. For example, some people claim that homosexuality is unnatural—it doesn't promote procreation as Nature intends sex to do—therefore homosexuality is bad. Among other problems with this jump in logic is that there are loads of examples of homosexual activity in nature, from barn owls to bison to bonobo monkeys. What's more, I have never met a homosexual who didn't believe his practices felt perfectly natural to him.

Greene does not fall victim to this fallacy. Still, he does believe that in order to come up with functional ideas and principles about how people *ought* to behave, it would be a good idea to find out how people actually *do* go about making moral decisions. What is that process and what informs it? And where did moral decision-making come from in the first place?

One question that psychologists and brain physiologists are now asking is: Is the human brain hardwired to make good moral choices? Is altruism, for example, built into our DNA? These thinkers suggest that, like physical characteristics, psychological characteristics evolved on the basis of survival of the fittest, and perhaps altruism evolved as a survival characteristic for our species—at least, for individual groups of our species.

Professor Joshua Greene, who has a background in both philosophy and psychology, is one of these thinkers. In that quote I copied into my notebook, Greene is pointing to a fundamental disconnect in our hardwiring: For very good survival reasons, we have evolved to look after our own—our own tribe—but we also evolved to fear and fight competing tribes. Altruism works terrifically in the neighborhood—an ethic of helping one's neighbor is good for the survival of everyone in the tribe. But outside of the tribe? Not so much. In fact, there are even gradations of altruism within the tribe. As the scientist J. B. S. Haldane dryly put it, "I would lay down my life for two brothers . . . or eight cousins."

The basic problem is that today members of different tribes run into one another all the time. National tribes, political tribes, religious tribes, gated-community tribes—you name it. These days it is hard to leave the house without encountering someone from a different tribe. And taking a plane trip or, for that matter, simply reading the newspaper, we encounter other tribe members everywhere. Greene concludes that the major problem of moral philosophy is to figure out how to bridge the gap between our tribal instincts and this multitribal world we live in.

Greene has an idea of how we may be able to do this, and in many ways it is basically the Utilitarianism of John Stuart Mill and Jeremy Bentham retooled to take into account recent discoveries on how we humans make our moral decisions.

First, we need to understand that we have two fundamentally different ways of making moral decisions: by way of fast, instinctive thought and by way of slow, deliberative thought. The former tends to be more emotional and the latter more rational. Obviously, the moral conclusions reached by each method are frequently at odds with each other. But one quality they have in common is this altruistic, Golden Rule–ish and utilitarian gut feeling that has evolved in us. In our fast, instinctive mode, we automatically apply our inborn altruism to our family and tribe. We instinctively desist from stealing from our kid's piggy bank (well, at least most of us do). No deep reasoning is needed in this case. In our slow, deliberative mode, we rationally determine that the Golden Rule makes good sense, but in this mode we try to apply it to *everybody*, not just members of our tribe—the greatest good for the greatest number of *all* people. We decide it would be wrong to steal from *anybody's* piggy bank, even if the owner of the piggy bank is a member of another tribe. But most of the time there is a tension between these two modes of decision-making that parallels the tension between our evolved tribal instincts and this multitribal world we live in.

No, Greene is not leading up to a proposition that we can realize a better world by suppressing our quick, instinctive moral mode and just go with our slow, contemplative mode. As he once wittily put it, "We wouldn't want to blindly condemn our moral intuitions with 'guilt by neural association.'" Anyway, he says, we are simply incapable of tossing away our "automatic settings." But he does think we have a chance at transcending them.

One way to do this is for us to get our two modes to talk to each other. Then, maybe our instinctive altruism can give some solid emotional ground to our thoughtful Utilitarianism, and our thoughtful Utilitarianism can give our instincts a push toward more inclusion. The rational principles of our contemplative mode may never feel comfortable to our instinctive selves, but what we do have going for us is that "everyone feels the pull of impartiality as a moral ideal." It is a modest step, this internal chat, but Greene thinks it could lead to a greater good.

I am impressed with Greene's practical approach to ethics and the modest, sober-minded goals that follow from it. Too often, moral philosophers are so estranged from the way people actually think and behave that their pronouncements sound like blowing in the wind.

I am also indebted to Greene for assuaging my guilt when I fail Peter Singer's moral fable tests. Writes Greene: "It's not reasonable to expect actual humans to put aside nearly everything they love for the sake of the greater good. Speaking for myself, I spend money on my children that would be better spent on distant starving children, and I have no intention of stopping. After all, I'm only human! But I'd rather be a human who knows that he's a hypocrite, and who tries to be less so, than one who mistakes his species-typical moral limitations for ideal values."

I'm good with that.

> "People deserve much less punishment, or even
> perhaps no punishment, for what they did many years ago
> as compared to with what they did very recently."
>
> ....
>
> —DEREK PARFIT, BRITISH PHILOSOPHER
> (1942–), ANALYTIC MORAL PHILOSOPHER

I HEARD ABOUT DEREK PARFIT FROM THE SAME SAVVY YOUNG student who had introduced me to the work of the techno-hedonist David Pearce. Both Parfit and Pearce come out of Oxford, both have boyish faces and great masses of unruly hair, and both possess over-the-top imaginations.

To demonstrate his ideas, Parfit often uses thought experiments, hypothetical scenarios that feel like wild mental roller-coaster rides. After my third or fourth hair-raising plunge down Parfit's roller-coaster tracks, I am usually ready to entertain just about *any* idea. Incidentally, I believe thought experiments are the most promising way contemporary philosophers are making philosophy attractive and accessible to all of us.

So fasten your seatbelts. Parfit's aim in the following thought experiment is to demonstrate that personal identity is a slippery thing at best, so questions of moral responsibility are far more complicated than we usually believe they are. Here goes:

"Suppose that you enter a cubicle in which, when you press a button, a scanner records the states of all the cells in your brain and body, destroying both while doing so. This information is then transmitted at the speed of light to some other planet, where a replicator produces a perfect organic copy of you. Since the brain of your Replica is exactly like yours, it will seem to remember living your life up to the moment when you pressed the button, its character will be just like yours, and it will be in every other way psychologically continuous with you."

Is this new "you" still you? Is this thing on Mars that thinks it is you any different from the thing that used to be you on Earth?

Philosophers make a distinction between *qualitative* differences and *numerical* differences. Two cars that are exactly the same model and color are numerically different but qualitatively identical. On the other hand, Superman and Clark Kent are qualitatively different but numerically identical—same guy, but with different qualities; Superman's ability to leap tall buildings in a single bound is not something Clark can do.

Parfit says the two yous in his thought experiment are clearly numerically different. Call the "you" who once existed on Earth You #1, and the one who now exists on Mars You #2. Count 'em: one, two. These two Yous are just like the two same-model, same-color cars. And as with those cars, this numerical difference makes no qualitative difference. If You #2 not only looks exactly like You #1 and has the same DNA as You #1, but also thinks he is You #1 in that he has all of You #1's personal memories and personality and character, then he is *identical* to You #1. Same guy. That is because personal memories and personality and character add up to the sum total of what a personal identity is. Try to think of what could possibly make the two Yous different from each other besides their numerical difference. I've tried. Can't do it.

This definition of personal identity raises some thorny ethical questions about who is responsible for what, starting with the question, Who's who? But before I get into these questions, fascinating as they are, I feel like playing some more of Parfit's Star-Trekian mind games. They are just too much fun to resist.

Here's one of my favorites, as written by one of Parfit's colleagues, George Vesey:

"Two men, a Mr. Brown and a Mr. Robinson, had been operated on for brain tumors and brain extractions had been performed on both of them. At the end of the operation, however, the assistant inadvertently put Brown's brain in Robinson's head, and Robinson's brain in Brown's head. One of these men immediately dies, but the other, the one with Robinson's body and Brown's brain, eventually regains consciousness. Let us call the latter 'Brownson.' Upon regaining consciousness Brownson exhibits great shock and surprise at the appearance of his body. Then, upon seeing Brown's body, he exclaims incredulously 'That's me lying there.' Pointing to himself he says 'This isn't my body; the one over there is.' When asked his name, he automatically says 'Brown.' He recognizes Brown's wife and family (whom Robinson had never met), and is able to describe in detail events in Brown's life, always describing them as events in his own life. Of Robinson's past life he evinces no knowledge at all. Over a period of time he is observed to display all of the personality traits, mannerisms, interests, likes and dislikes, and so on, that had previously characterized Brown, and to act and talk in ways completely alien to the old Robinson."

So who, exactly, survived the operation and who did not?

Again, Parfit believes that over time personal identity is nothing more than what he calls "psychological continuity," all those ongoing memories, personality traits, mannerisms, interests, and so on that make Brown *Brown*, whatever body he happens to be inhabiting. That's it. Personal identity is nothing else—*not*, say, a particular material object or, at the other end of the spectrum, some kind of a metaphysical entity like a soul.

One of my favorite Sardar jokes perfectly illustrates Parfit's distinction between self-as-an-object and self-as-psychological-continuity (in Indian humor, Sardars are stereotypically literal-minded to the point of ridiculousness):

> *Riding on the train to Mumbai, a Sardar wants to take a nap but does not want to miss his station, so he asks the compartment's other occupant to wake him up when they get*

*close to Mumbai. He tells this fellow that he will give him
100 rupees for this service.*

*Well, the other fellow feels that 100 rupees is a lot of
money just for waking up the Sardar so, being a barber by
profession, he decides to give the snoozing Sardar a little
something extra for his money. While the man sleeps, the
barber gives him a good trim and a clean shave, removing his
entire beard.*

*When they approach Mumbai, the barber wakes the
Sardar and gets his payment. The Sardar gets off the train
and goes to his apartment where he goes to the bathroom to
wash up. Looking in the mirror he becomes furious—"That
son of a bitch! I gave him 100 rupees and he woke up the
wrong man!"*

Sometimes Parfit's thought experiments make me think he
should consider writing fantasy film scripts as a backup profession.
And speaking of Hollywood, here is my all-time favorite Parfit
scenario:

"Imagine that Derek Parfit is being gradually transformed molecule by molecule into Greta Garbo. At the beginning of this
whole process there's Derek Parfit, then at the end of the whole
process it's really clear that Derek Parfit no longer exists. Derek
Parfit is gone. Now there's Greta Garbo. Now, the key question is
this: At what point along this transformation did the change take

place? When did Derek cease to exist and when did Greta come to exist? If you just have to reflect on this question for a while, immediately it becomes clear that there couldn't be some single point—there couldn't be a single second, say—in which Derek stops existing and Greta starts existing. What you're seeing is some kind of gradual process where, as this person becomes more and more and more different from the Derek that we know now, it becomes less and less right to say that he's Derek at all and more and more right to say that he is gone and a completely other person has come into existence."

Parfit's point in the Garbo fantasy is that personal identity is a *matter of degree*, as in "now more Garbo than Parfit." Analogously, in our real, non-thought-experiment lives, our memories of our experiences, including memories of past thoughts and feelings, are also a matter of degree. They are on a scale of weak to strong. So it seems reasonable to say that our weak memories constitute less of our personal identity than do our strong memories. Likewise, our convictions and tastes.

In short, it is an illusion to think of identity as a static, absolute phenomenon as we usually do because ultimately identity is a matter of degree—it's all relative. When my wife says to me, "You aren't the man I married," Parfit would say that she is on to something. At some point, in fact, if I became more Garbo than Danny, she would definitely have legitimate grounds for leaving me—well, not exactly leaving *me*.

Now back to that quote of Parfit's which I recently jotted down in my "Pithies" notebook: "People deserve much less punishment, or even perhaps no punishment, for what they did many years ago as compared to with what they did very recently."

The idea here is that many years ago, someone—say, someone called Ralphy—was not entirely the same person he is today. For example, today Ralphy may have totally forgotten that time he forged his brother's signature on a check and got away with it. In the intervening years, Ralphy may have become an upstanding citizen. *Or not.* It doesn't really matter; Parfit is not suggesting some kind of forgive-and-forget morality. He is simply saying that over time, what with his waxing and waning of memories and convictions, Ralphy has become a significantly different person. So what sense would it make to punish this "new" Ralphy for something the "old" Ralphy did so many years ago? Yes, there is clearly some relationship between these two Ralphies, but with the passage of time, that relationship has become weaker and weaker to the point where punishing one for the other's crime does not make good sense.

That conclusion certainly is hard to buy. In fact, Parfit's reasoning is so counterintuitive that it can easily sound trivial and goofy, like a late-night theory spun by a stoner. That was my first impression. But then I tried to find a rigorous and rational concept of personal identity that was more than just psychological continuity. Not easy. Slippery thing, being a "me."

———

Apparently, Parfit is still in flux about the nature of personal identity. Many years after writing *Reasons and Persons*, he wrote an essay with the provocative title "We Are Not Human Beings," in which he suggested that numerical differences (the You #1 and You #2 in the Mars transporter scenario) *are* significant after all. The question then seems to be, is the man who wrote "We Are Not Human Beings" the same person who wrote *Reasons and Persons*?

Parfit's ultimate goal—the one to which he has dedicated his life—is to find a rational foundation for ethics. He wants to discover a moral principle that is as true and defensible as the principles of logic and science. This puts him in a lonely position, to say the least. In the past hundred years, since Logical Positivists like Bertrand Russell and A. J. Ayer have argued that the idea of a rational basis for ethics is as impossible as a rational basis for the existence of God—or of the Tooth Fairy, for that matter—Parfit's goal has been pretty much off the philosophical table.

But Parfit soldiered on. In 2011, after years of solitary noodling, he published a two-volume essay on moral philosophy called *On What Matters*. In it, he puts forth what he calls his Triple Theory of ethics that combines traditional philosophy's main ethical theories to form a rational, objective basis for morality. Parfit claims that rather than disagree with one another, these theories converge, as if "climbing the same mountain on different sides."

Needless to mention, his Triple Theory is beyond me and shall remain so for the rest of my molecular life, but many philosophers—especially younger ones—believe that Parfit is on to something that will revolutionize ethics. I wish them well.

While Parfit was frantically putting together the proofs of *On What Matters* for an upcoming lecture in the United States, he collapsed. A doctor diagnosed him with "transient global amnesia." Since that time, Parfit occasionally breaks down in uncontrollable weeping. Perhaps, at the age of seventy-two, Parfit is overwhelmed by the idea that he may not come up with an irrefutable moral theory before he dies.

But it is not death itself he fears. He recently wrote: "Consider the fact that, in a few years, I shall be dead. This fact can seem depressing. But the reality is only this. After a certain time, none of the thoughts and experiences that occur will be directly causally related to this brain, or be connected in certain ways to these present experiences. That is all this fact involves. And, in that description, my death seems to disappear."

I have to wonder if somewhere deep down Parfit cannot fully accept his concept of personal identity and the cool, objective view of his own mortality that follows from it. Maybe that is where his uncontrollable tears come from. Nonetheless, his fabulous thought experiments and the questions they raise remain eternally dazzling.

LUDWIG WITTGENSTEIN ONCE SAID, "A SERIOUS AND GOOD PHILO-sophical work could be written consisting entirely of jokes." Seems like a good idea to me, although those qualifiers "serious" and "good" sound daunting.

The above gag from the late, much-revered Harvard philosopher George Santayana is one of my all-time favorite philogags. Like most good philosophical jokes, it contains a paradox: Something both *is* and *isn't* at the same time—no God, but, hey, this nonexistent being has a mother. It reminds me of that wonderful Yogi Berra–ism about a St. Louis restaurant: "Nobody goes there anymore, it's so crowded."

In paradoxes, we get to have things both ways: We can be both a believer and a nonbeliever in one breath. Of course, we also get to be neither, because the two prongs of the paradox cancel each other out. Not all paradoxes are conceived of as jokes, but nonetheless they tend to strike us as funny, as counterintuitive incongruities tend to do. A favorite of philosophers is one based on

Bertrand Russell's paradox and known as the Barber Paradox: "In a town where the sole barber, a man, shaves all the male citizens of the town who do not shave themselves, does the barber shave himself?" Makes me laugh.

Santayana, a student of William James, was known as a wit. He was also known as a man whose life informed his philosophy and vice versa. He once said that he stood in philosophy "exactly where he stood in daily life." In daily life, he tried to balance a belief in the human spirit and atheism. As a nonpracticing Catholic, he said, "My affection for the Catholic system is justified naturalistically because I regard it as a true symbol for the real relations of spirit within nature."

Subtle stuff. For me, his paradoxical Mary gag nails it better.

> "The soul of the wise dwells in the house of mourning,
> but the soul of fools dwells in the house of pleasure."
>
> ....
>
> —ECCLESIASTES (OLD TESTAMENT),
>
> THIRD CENTURY BC, AUTHOR UNKNOWN

PHILOSOPHICALLY MINDED PEOPLE WHO STUBBORNLY KEEP wrestling with the how-to-live question often end up dipping into the Holy Bible on the chance that they'll find a clue or two there. We also take the occasional plunge into the Koran, the Upanishads, the Bhagavad Gita, the Lotus Sutra, and, always fun on a mellow evening with good friends, the I Ching. God knows, these sacred texts have satisfactorily answered the big questions for most people, so it would be foolhardy to ignore them. Plus, a great number of the major philosophers base some of their principles on these texts, so to get the backstory on their ideas some scripture-dipping makes good sense.

But that said, it is always hard for me to find inspiring clues, let alone comfort, when I open the Bible to the "Writings" section and read the poetic rant of Ecclesiastes, the Teacher. Especially that part where the Teacher says:

"Meaningless! Meaningless! Utterly meaningless! Everything is meaningless!"

Oy!

Nothing a person does has any lasting or transcendental value, the Teacher goes on. Life is simply vanity—emptiness—and then, by God (literally), it's over. This is probably the earliest iteration of the modern T-shirt legend: "Life sucks and then you die."

Scholars are still unsure who exactly this disenchanted Teacher was. Some evidence points to King Solomon, but the bleak rhetoric of the Teacher doesn't seem to jibe with the rest of Solomon's teachings, heretical as these sometimes could be. In the original ancient Hebrew, Ecclesiastes's narrator was called *Qoheleth*, which has been variously translated as "Speaker," "Preacher," and "Philosopher." By any name, this was a man to be reckoned with.

The only human quality the Teacher gives any credit is wisdom, although it is not entirely clear what one would do with wisdom in a meaningless life—perhaps come to grips with the idea that life is meaningless. Maybe this accounts for our greater likelihood of acquiring wisdom in the House of Mourning.

Still, there have been periods in my life when this "wisdom in the House of Mourning" message profoundly resonated with me and that is why the Teacher's message found its way into my notebook. Those periods have been when I suffered a terrible personal loss and grieved intensely. At those times, I frequently felt some kind of enlightenment at the bottom of my depths of feeling. I felt that I was finally facing a fundamental fact of life: that everything is transient and loss is inevitable; that is just the way it is. Since most of the time

I try to ignore this immutable fact, finally embracing it bore the sweetness of embracing Truth. And embracing that truth, painful as it is, can make me feel more authentically alive. *Life's losses are awful, yet somehow I can accept them and carry on.*

But at other times—perhaps more superficially lived times—I feel just the opposite. I find the Teacher's admonition to feel bad because it is good for me totally demoralizing. I admit that one reason the Teacher's precept distresses me is rather trivial: As a boy, when I asked if I could go out and play after dinner, my mother often replied, "No, you've had enough fun for today!" Mom's implication was that too much fun was bad for me, that it would make me worthless. Take that, ye who are considering a life of pure pleasure!

And if the Teacher's implication is that there is absolutely no wisdom available outside the walls of the House Mourning, I've had it with him. It is one thing to hear that good times make me unworthy, but it is even more disheartening to hear that good times make me stupid.

Still, as I read on, the Teacher does allow that life is better than death, which is a relief of sorts. And the Teacher even goes so far as to hint that making the most of our short, meaningless time here is worth a try.

No uplift in this chapter of the Bible. I certainly have gone through periods of my life when I felt overwhelmed by the meaninglessness of it all, but I never felt the need to advertise it, as the Teacher does. It certainly is not a lesson I ever felt the urge to pass on to my daughter or granddaughter.

And therein lies a realization I had recently: Even in my darkest moments, I cannot think of my daughter's life or my granddaughter's life as meaningless. Their mere existence feels meaningful to me whenever I think about them. How could such vital and beautiful creatures possibly be insignificant? Yes, these are the sentimental thoughts of an old codger, but do take note, Teacher.

> "Religion is the one endeavor in which us/them thinking achieves a transcendent significance. If you really believe that calling God by the right name can spell the difference between eternal happiness and eternal suffering, then it becomes quite reasonable to treat heretics and unbelievers rather badly. The stakes of our religious differences are immeasurably higher than those born of mere tribalism, racism, or politics."

....

—SAM HARRIS, AMERICAN PHILOSOPHER (1967–), ATHEIST

I HAPPENED TO READ SAM HARRIS'S SEMINAL BOOK *THE END OF Faith: Religion, Terror, and the Future of Reason* only weeks before the Twin Towers were destroyed, but it was not until after that atrocity that I copied the above paragraph into my notebook. I was convinced beyond doubt that Harris was right: Organized religion is the primary scourge of our time.

Sam Harris, the late Christopher Hitchens, and the contemporary British philosopher Richard Dawkins composed what one wag calls the Holy Trinity of the New Atheism. Harris and Dawkins continue to write books and articles, give speeches, and engage in public debates to declaim the irrationality of religious beliefs and to warn that religion is the source of most of our societal woes. They believe that religion is behind virtually all of today's deadliest wars.

Harris nails the source of the problem with his mocking line, "Calling God by the right name can spell the difference between eternal happiness and eternal suffering." If your belief system is different from mine, you are my enemy because we cannot both be right. The reason both cannot be right is that we apply the basic law of reason, the law of noncontradiction (something cannot be true and not true in the same sense at the same time), to faith and its objects. This makes any alternative belief system a threat to one's own and, as this is a threat to life's supreme prize, eternal happiness, it needs to be eliminated.

All sadly true, but recently I have begun to think Harris is being parochial when he claims that "religion is the *one* endeavor in which us/them thinking achieves a transcendent significance." Hate-inducing belief systems are not limited to religions. Fervid nationalism induces mass murder all over the world, always has; and in that nationalism is a product of an absolute belief system, it, too, can be seen as having "transcendent significance." Competing politico-economic ideologies also instigate hate and bloodshed. And indeed, so do tribalism and racism. I do not think it is either wise or productive to weigh one atrocity against another, to claim that one mass murder precipitate is more deadly than another.

What all these hate-mongering systems have in common is that their true believers are unwilling to say, "Your belief system works for you, mine works for me, so let us just go on our merry, separate ways." They cannot accept a *relativity* of belief systems because for them a belief system must be *absolutely* true, otherwise it would not have absolute value. There can only be one god; his name is Yahweh (or Allah, or Vishnu, or whatever) and all other "gods" are false. There can only be one valid world economic system and that is communism (or pure market capitalism, or utopian socialism, or whatever).

As the New Atheists win converts, I have noticed a new form of religious intolerance gaining steam: nonbelievers trashing religion itself, sometimes putting down believers up close and personal. Recently, a good friend of mine attended an Orthodox Jewish wedding of one of his relatives. As is the tradition in Orthodox services and celebrations, men and women both prayed and danced separately from one another. My friend took offense on feminist grounds and voiced his objections at the wedding. He did not approve of their practices and felt he needed to let them know that. This is hardly opening gunfire or even throwing stones, but it is still intolerance. It is still "my belief system is superior to yours."

Throughout my life, I have heard people claim that religion is the refuge of simpletons, the "opiate of the masses." When I am in the company of bright, well-educated people who generally consider themselves fair and open-minded, I notice that they often refer to religious people as simple folk who are deluding themselves in order to fulfill a psychological need, and they assume the present company agrees. In short, they take for granted that atheism is the "one true religion." This bothers me as much as listening to some smug evangelical zealot hold forth on *his* one true religion. We agnostics are funny that way.

Fortunately, Harris does make a crucial distinction between religion and mysticism. While religion inevitably leads to absolutism and us/them polarization, mysticism can exist as a private matter. It does not need to be shared with like-minded people, compared to alternative systems, or made public in any way. And it most certainly does not need to lead to hatred and war.

So what exactly is mysticism? That master of conciseness Ludwig Wittgenstein sums it up beautifully: "Mysticism wonders not *how* the world is but *that* the world is."

> "A little philosophy inclineth man's mind to atheism, but depth in philosophy bringeth men's minds about to religion."
>
> ....
>
> —FRANCIS BACON, ENGLISH PHILOSOPHER
> AND SCIENTIST (1561–1626)

I MAY BE UNQUALIFIED TO SHED MUCH LIGHT ON THIS ONE because I have never been able to dig down to the deepest reaches of philosophy. I tend to get bogged down—not to mention, claustrophobic—in the subsoil of "extensional logic" and "epistemic contextualism." (*Don't ask what these are—Please!*) Yet this does not stop me from being fascinated by Bacon's pronouncement every time I think about it. And at times I do get a potent whiff of what he meant.

Aristotle famously said, "The more you know, the more you know you don't know," and Bacon is picking up from there. Admitting to ourselves how little we know and, more significantly, how little is even knowable, can be a real eye-opener. There is an awful lot of unknowable stuff out there, but somehow that does not keep us from wanting to know about it or, at least, to keep wondering about it. And wondering about the unknowable certainly inclineth a mind toward the spiritual.

Many of my whiffs of Bacon's meaning come when I think about the division of philosophy known as epistemology, theories of knowledge. Epistemology asks the question, "What is knowable?" For example, the eighteenth-century British Empiricist George Berkeley makes the case that all our knowledge of the world comes to us through our senses, so in the end all we've really got is this sense data inside our heads. We cannot claim that is a chair *out there*, only that we have some chair sense data in our minds. So it is impossible to claim that the chair is anything more than a bunch of sensory experiences that we cobble together in our minds and call a "chair." Berkeley put it succinctly and dramatically when he stated, *"Esse est precipi"* ("to be is to be perceived").

I can still remember how Berkeley's statement struck me when I first heard it in a college lecture. I thought: *Here we go again— more pointless philosophical games! Maybe Dad was right, I should be studying something practical, like mechanical engineering—at least then I could* build *a chair.*

But that evening, going over my lecture notes, I had an *Aha!* moment. Berkeley wasn't playing games—he was just telling it like it is: An object's existence *is* simply a perception, end of story. We can't creep out from behind our senses and in some other way *know* that there is an object "out there." So, really, all we can mean when we say that an object exists is that some sense data resides inside our heads. If minds really do boggle, mine did.

But then Berkeley let me down. He had to account for where this sense data comes from and, being a Christian bishop, he argued that it must come from God, who is issuing sense data from on high from some kind of divine master computer. That is where he lost me; his guy-in-the-sky explanation bringeth not my mind to religion.

Yet he does get me thinking in a fanciful sort of way. If all I have got is sense data, maybe what I believe exists is severely limited by the sense organs I come equipped with. (Remember, I am thinking fancifully here.) So if I literally had a sixth sense, maybe more things would exist for me—maybe something godlike, such as, for example, God. Maybe an entirely new dimension would open up to me. Suddenly, my mind starts to bring me toward at least the outskirts of religion. People who have had religious experiences via yoga or mind-altering drugs make claims like this: A new sense was brought to life inside them and with it came the perception of new entities, some of which appeared to be holy entities.

I asked Tom for his take on Bacon's quote. Although Tom spent many years in divinity school, he insisted that Bacon's pronouncement was above his pay grade, but, as always, he did have some interesting ideas about it.

For one thing, he said, if you are a skeptical philosopher who subjects everything to a strict test of reason, God is only *one* of many things that don't make the grade. A philosopher engaged in radical doubt ends up with only sense data and the rules of logic on the table—or rather, on that configuration of sense data that we call a "table." But that's all, folks. Gone with God are also all moral principles; in the end there is no rational way to prove that any action is good or bad, so off the table morality should go, too. Ultimately, we take our belief in good and evil on faith, pretty much the same way some people take their belief in God. So the question is: Are we willing to throw out our faith in morality along with our faith in God? After all, one is as irrational as the other. And if not—if we *are* willing to make an exception to our faith-scuttling in the case of moral principles—why exactly don't we also make an exception in the case of the existence of God?

Or, Tom said, maybe Bacon meant that eventually philosophy leads us to the conclusion that life is absurd and meaningless. After all, if we cannot prove that anything is of value, it's impossible to make the case that life itself has any value. This is the point where some philosophers, like Søren Kierkegaard, say that they just can't go on living a life that has no meaning, so strict rationality be damned. He decides to give his life meaning himself, starting with an irrational belief in God. He takes an irrational leap of faith.

I am still trying to keep an open mind about this stuff, but I am not getting any younger, and, as a friend of mine once said, "Don't forget that when an agnostic dies, he goes on to the Great Perhaps."

> "I saw a Divine Being. I'm afraid I'm going to have to revise all my various books and opinions."
>
> ....
>
> —A. J. AYER, BRITISH PHILOSOPHER
> (1910–1989), LOGICAL POSITIVIST

WHEN I READ THESE WORDS FROM PROFESSOR AYER IN 1988 IN A newspaper clipping sent to me by a friend living in London, I couldn't believe my eyes—a serious problem for an empiricist. Ayer was known as one of the most skeptical epistemologists in the history of philosophy. What in God's name was going on here?

At the age of twenty, after reading Ayer's seminal book *Language, Truth, and Logic,* I was so overwhelmed that I curled up on my bed in the fetal position. Ayer had systematically torn apart just about everything I thought I knew and, more significantly, what I thought I *could* know. Damned little, he said.

In lucid prose, Ayer laid out the fundamentals of Logical Positivism, establishing the limits of what we can meaningfully talk about. That, he said, is only stuff that is demonstrably either true or false. Logical and mathematical propositions can be verified or disproved by analysis, so these made the cut. *"Two and two equals*

four?" "Yes, that checks out." And empirical propositions about the
existence, properties, and movements of things in the real world
can be verified or disproved by observation, so these are meaningful also. *"Is that an apple tree over there?" "Yup, on close inspection,
a tree bearing apples it is."*

But that is it, the limit of certain knowledge.

Forget about making meaningful propositions about what is
good or bad, beautiful or ugly, worthwhile or worthless. There is
no way to verify whether such propositions are true or false, so they
are, well, *worthless*—at least as far as rational discourse is concerned. Ayer wrote that to say something is "bad"—such as, "Hitting
somebody on the head is bad"—means no more than saying "ouch"
when somebody hits *you* on the head. Neither are verifiable propositions; they are just expressions of how the speaker feels. Ditto for
saying that the *Mona Lisa* is a great work of art. And, of course, the
proposition that "Life is meaningful" has no meaning; there is no way
to verify or disprove it.

Suddenly, the subjects that philosophy could meaningfully talk
about were toppling like tenpins. Ooops, there go Ethics and Aes-
thetics. And, good God, there go Religion and Theology along
with all the other metaphysical subjects that philosophers had been
debating for the past couple thousand years. Philosophers and philosophy students all over the map were assuming the fetal position,
moaning, "Is that all there is?" But they could not come up with a

rational argument to refute Logical Positivism. All they were left with were those messy, amorphous things called feelings, and from feelings alone comes not rigorous philosophy.

For such a cynical fellow, A. J. Ayer (known as Freddie to his friends) was affable and gregarious. And for such a nerdy-looking scholar, he seemed to be quite the lady's man; in addition to his four successive marriages to three refined British ladies (he married one of them twice), he managed to squeeze in an affair with the glamorous Hollywood gossip columnist Sheilah Graham, with whom he fathered a daughter. As it happened, Ayer himself turned up in the gossip columns at the age of seventy-seven when he confronted the boxer Mike Tyson at a Manhattan cocktail party. As the story goes, Freddie was chatting with some fashion designers and models when they heard a guest screaming that her friend was being assaulted in the bedroom. Ayer sprang into action: He rushed to the bedroom, where he found Tyson forcing himself on the yet unknown young model Naomi Campbell. He told the boxer to cut it out. Immediately!

Responded Tyson: "Do you know who the fuck I am? I'm the heavyweight champion of the world!"

Replied Ayer: "And I am the former Wykeham Professor of Logic. We are both pre-eminent in our field; I suggest that we talk about this like rational men."

Witnesses say that Ayer and Tyson then discussed some relevant ethical issues, although wisely Ms. Campbell decamped before the debate reached a conclusion.

Freddie reveled in being a public figure, appearing frequently on BBC programs to hold forth on all the ridiculous beliefs held by so-called intelligent people—such as beliefs in God and an afterlife. In Great Britain, Ayer was considered the Atheist-in-Chief, although he preferred to call himself an "igtheist"—one who maintains that the very idea of "God" is devoid of meaning. On radio and television, he engaged in numerous debates with the most notable bishops and theologians of the land, famously giving a good intellectual drubbing to the erudite Jesuit Priest Frederick Copleston. (*Remember that name—Frederick Copleston.*)

Twenty-five years after reading *Language, Truth, and Logic*, although I no longer curled up in despondency when I thought about Ayer's no-holds-barred skepticism, it still gave me the willies. In any event, at around the same time as the Tyson incident I came across an interview in the *London Observer* in which Ayer said, "It seems that I have spent my entire time trying to make life more rational and that it was all wasted effort."

How's that again, A.J.?

Ayer's colleagues, quietly bemused, insisted that Ayer really wasn't devaluing his life's work, he was merely gesturing to the fact there are other things in life besides the subjects that philosophers talk about. Like, perhaps, feelings—say, feelings of righteous indignation when you come upon a man attempting to rape a woman.

Less than a year after the *Observer* interview, Ayer had a near-death experience, the result, he later wrote, of a chunk of tuna that he "carelessly tossed" down his gullet. Ayer's detailed description of "What I Saw When I Was Dead" (the title of the article he wrote about his experience) would make a nifty screenplay for a supernatural thriller. Here are a few highlights:

"It was most extraordinary. My thoughts became persons."

And,

"I was confronted by a red light. . . . Aware that this light was responsible for the government of the universe. Among its ministers were two creatures who had been put in charge of space . . . that space, like a badly fitted jigsaw puzzle, was slightly out of joint . . . with the consequence that the laws of nature had ceased to function as they should."

Ayer wrote that he then realized that it was his personal responsibility to set things right by making certain adjustments to Time in the Time-Space Continuum. In short, you had to be there to understand what he was talking about, but Ayer most certainly was *there*.

Understandably, Ayer's account caused a furor in the world of philosophy. Was the old logician drifting into dementia? As with many another mortal, had the prospect of his impending death clouded his mind? Indeed, Ayer, himself, did a little backtracking, saying that his otherworldly experiences "have weakened, not my belief that there is no life after death, but my inflexible attitude towards that belief." That's philosophy talk for "I'm giving myself a little wiggle room here."

But here is the part of Ayer's story that inclines me toward wonder—spiritual wonder. A BBC correspondent named Peter Foges, who knew Ayer well, talked with one Dr. George, the physician who attended Ayer immediately after his near-death experience. Reported Foges: "'[Ayer] clearly said "Divine Being,"'" said Dr. George. 'He was confiding in me, and I think he was slightly embarrassed because it was unsettling for him as an atheist. He spoke in a very confidential manner. I think he felt he had come face to face with God, or his maker, or what one might say was God.'"

Publicly, Ayer kept downplaying his otherworldly encounter, but Foges writes that privately, the atheist-in-chief had clearly changed: "'He became so much nicer after he died,' was the sardonic way Dee Wells [a former wife] put it. 'He was not nearly so boastful. He took an interest in other people.' . . . What she also noticed is that as his life ebbed away, Ayer began spending a great deal of time with Father Frederick Copleston, his former opponent in the BBC debate. Until then they'd never been particularly close, though Ayer had grudging respect for Copleston's muscular mind. . . . Nevertheless, in the last year of his life, Ayer spent many hours in Copleston's company, talking and arguing about who knows what. They must have made an odd couple seated together in the darkest recesses of London's Garrick Club. The Catholic divine even graced

Ayer's scrupulously secular cremation. 'In the end, he was Freddie's closest friend,' said Dee. 'It was quite extraordinary.'"

Maybe Francis Bacon had it wrong—at least in Ayer's case. Instead of finding meaning in religion as the result of studying philosophy in depth, Ayer found that meaning by not thinking like a philosopher at all for a few divine moments.

As an agnostic who still hopes that someday, somehow, I will catch my own glimpse of a Divine Being, I cannot help but take comfort in the fact that this brilliant, skeptical philosopher saw one himself. I am all too ready to have my hitherto "inflexible doubts" weakened.

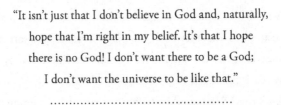

"It isn't just that I don't believe in God and, naturally, hope that I'm right in my belief. It's that I hope there is no God! I don't want there to be a God; I don't want the universe to be like that."

....

—THOMAS NAGEL, AMERICAN PHILOSOPHER
(1937–), ETHICIST AND SOCIAL PHILOSOPHER

I HAVE TO ADMIT THAT THERE IS SOMETHING REFRESHING ABOUT a man who not only embraces atheism, but would be mighty relieved if atheism could be proven true. He is just the opposite of most of us agnostics who would be relieved if something came along to prove that God *does* exist. That, it turns out, is most agnostics' highest hope, our dirty little secret. What is more, we are getting damned tired of sitting on the fence all the time. Hoping for a proof of atheism sounds a lot less taxing. That is the reason I jotted down Nagel's lines: Endlessly ruminating about faith yet never experiencing it can take its toll. I wanted to think about what Nagel's attitude toward faith had to offer as an alternative.

Nagel's argument begins with what he calls our "fear of religion," a fear with which he claims to be personally familiar. By this, he does not mean the fear that the New Atheists talk about—a fear based on the observation that religion can corrupt society, make us despise those who do not share our religious beliefs, and ultimately make us kill one another. That may be so, but Nagel is referring to something else, something fundamental to the human condition. He says that what we basically fear is that *religion may be true.*

How's that? What could possibly be scary about religion being true?

Nagel says, "[T]he fear of religion may extend far beyond the existence of a personal god to include any cosmic order of which the mind is an irreducible and non-accidental part." By "irreducible and non-accidental," he means a mind that cannot be reduced to, say, randomly bouncing atoms, but one that is a unique and self-contained component of some universal order. We fear this scenario because ultimately we will not be able to comprehend that universal order, let alone what our irreducible and nonaccidental part in it is. The reason we will not be able to comprehend this infinite cosmic order is that we would be a finite part of it. Says Nagel, "We seem to be left with a question that has no imaginable answer: How is it possible for finite beings like us to think infinite thoughts?"

Nagel believes that if we know for certain that there *is* some kind of cosmic order out there—some kind of guiding principle or design—but we also know that our minds cannot possibly grasp what it is, we will be overwhelmed with frustration.

It is at this point where Nagel loses me. Yes, I do spend time wondering if, in good faith, I could make a Kierkegaardian leap of faith. And yes, I do grasp that a finite mind cannot possibly make sense of an infinite cosmic order. But such abstract apprehensions don't hit me in the gut. They are just too far removed, too heady, to get anywhere in the vicinity of my belly. I suspect only philosophers who are deeply immersed in abstruse thought—philosophers like Nagel—would be overwhelmed with this state of affairs. Most of us manage to live with all kinds of puzzles and mysteries on a daily basis—like, why did Paul die young while Frank, with all his bad traits, is still going strong at eighty? Such thoughts are upsetting and perplexing, but they do not make me howl over the inherent limitations of my understanding. Such puzzles and mysteries just make me lament the unfairness of life.

More to Nagel's point, I live with the fact that I don't know if there really is any meaningful cosmic order and, God knows, that is a continual frustration. But I don't understand why it should be any more frustrating to know that there *is* a grand design but I am unable to understand it. In both cases, I am in the cosmic dark.

Postscript: As a preamble to his "I hope there is no God" passage, Nagel wrote that "[I] am made uneasy by the fact that some of the most intelligent and well-informed people I know are religious believers."

I, too, know a great number of very bright and knowledgeable people who are believers. It sometimes makes me wonder if the skeptics have it backward: maybe I am just not *wise* enough to be a believer.

> "On this mountain the Lord Almighty will prepare
> a feast of rich food for all peoples,
> a banquet of aged wine—
> the best of meats and the finest of wines.
> On this mountain he will destroy
> the shroud that enfolds all peoples,
> the sheet that covers all nations;
> he will swallow up death forever.
> The Sovereign Lord will wipe away the tears
> from all faces;
> he will remove his people's disgrace
> from all the earth.
> The Lord has spoken."
>
> ....
>
> —ISAIAH, 25: 6–8 (OLD TESTAMENT)

ONE OF THE MOST INTELLIGENT AND KNOWLEDGEABLE RELIGIOUS believers in my life was my late father-in-law, Jan Vuijst, a Protestant minister and Old Testament scholar. When I first met him in Holland, he was disappointed to discover that his Jewish prospective son-in-law could not read the Old Testament in Hebrew as he did. I decided not to disappoint him further by informing him that I only rarely read the Old Testament even in English.

Nonetheless, this section of the Old Testament has a special resonance for me, one that involves my father-in-law, a man I grew to love and respect.

At a recent memorial service in Holland, a minister recalled a sermon on this section given by my father-in-law:

"I don't remember many sermons from my student time," this minister said, "but I do remember one by Jan Vuijst about this section of Isaiah and the discussion afterward. A member of the congregation asked: 'Pastor, is that really *all* that we can expect: just sitting with everybody on a mountaintop and eating and drinking?' Oh, no, I thought, how's he going to answer that one? At which point Jan Vuijst said: 'Yes, that is all. A feast for all people, in peace and abundance, with God as host—what more could you ask for?'"

Apart from any sentimental connection to my father-in-law, I really do get something meaningful out of his response.

Lately, I have begun to understand that many sophisticated believers use Bible talk because they think it is their best available option for expressing spiritual ideas and phenomena. They are the first to admit that this Bible talk is woefully inadequate, that it can only approximate what they are trying to understand and communicate. Like Nagel, they know that attempting to comprehend and express the infinite with a finite mind just isn't going to happen. But unlike Nagel, they try to do their best with what they have got. And one thing they have is the Bible. So when they quote a passage like this from Isaiah, they are using it as a unique kind of metaphor.

Many modern philosophers would say that they are on a hopeless track; you cannot use a metaphor from the immanent, finite world to shed any kind of light on a transcendental, infinite world—that is, if there were a transcendental, infinite world in the first place. There is just an unbridgeable disconnect between the finite and the infinite, so you cannot say anything, metaphorical or not, that has any meaning.

Point taken, but nevertheless every once in a while I do try to understand what these biblical metaphors *might* mean.

Isaiah, one of the major prophets in the Old Testament, preaches about the coming time of the messiah, so he figures prominently in Christian theology. Many Christian thinkers believe that although Christ made his appearance, the true Messianic Age is not here yet. To begin with, if that age were here, the world would not still be such a mess. And there are some Christian thinkers who believe that the Messianic Age is not even something of this world, that it is not an event in our future as we think of the future—not like, say, next Tuesday or some approaching age when computers will rule the world. No, the Messianic Age is something far more abstract, something way out there beyond Time and Space as we know it. My father-in-law was one of those thinkers.

When he responded that sitting around on the mountaintop eating and drinking with God is as good as it gets, that it is "all we could ask for," I believe he was saying, "You know, that's only a metaphor for something that is inexpressible in itself, but it's actually a damned good metaphor. Think about those rare moments in our lives when we are sitting around a table with the people we love. Think of the peacefulness and affection we feel at those moments. It feels like something holy is sitting there with us."

Three years ago, a late-night throbbing pain in my midsection sent me to the emergency room of my local hospital. A scan revealed that my appendix was on the verge of bursting and they sent me off to a hospital in a nearby city where they were equipped to do surgery. My wife drove. There, they wheeled me into an examination room where I promptly conked out.

Suddenly, I was standing out of doors on a lovely day, a small group of people on either side of me. None of us spoke. I felt wonderfully peaceful.

Just like in the movies, I then heard people shouting my name, and saw a rude light beaming through my eyelids. Very reluctantly, I opened my eyes. There were the doctors and my wife hovering over me. In the moment, I yearned to be back in that serene outdoor scene.

I doubt very much that this was a near-death experience. It certainly wasn't so elaborate or mind-blowing as Professor Ayer's tuna episode. No deity made an appearance. But the plain peacefulness that I experienced remains vivid in my memory. For a moment, all the tears had been wiped from my face.

> "When I consider the short duration of my life, swallowed up in the eternity before and after, the little space which I fill, and even can see, engulfed in the infinite immensity of spaces of which I am ignorant, and which know me not, I am frightened, and am astonished at being here rather than there; for there is no reason why here rather than there, why now rather than then. Who has put me here? By whose order and direction have this place and time been allotted to me?"
>
> ....
>
> —BLAISE PASCAL, FRENCH MATHEMATICIAN AND PHILOSOPHER (1623–1662), RATIONALIST AND CHRISTIAN BELIEVER

HOW ABOUT THAT! THERE WAS AN ETERNITY THAT *PRECEDED* MY life, not just one that comes after it. How could that have slipped my mind? That particular chunk of eternity does not seem to figure in most people's dread of nothingness. I yearn with all my heart for my life to continue evermore, yet I do not lose a moment's sleep over the fact that I missed the eternity before my birth. Is it simply a failure of imagination that allows me to face this "before" eternity without fear and trembling?

That was the question that prompted me to save this quote.

But in these lines from his *Pensées*, Pascal, a celebrated genius in his own time (he invented the first mechanical calculator in the mid-seventeenth century), is taking a leap of imagination that goes far beyond this before-and-after eternities phenomenon. He is performing a fantastic thought experiment with Time and Space: Why does he exist *now* instead of at some other time? Why is he *here* rather than in some other place?

Why, indeed? Is his existence here and now predetermined by natural events? By divine design? Or could it be totally arbitrary and therefore presumably without any purpose?

In his famous "wager," Pascal came down on the side of faith in God as Man's best bet: If Man turns out to be right in his faith, he has everything to gain; if he turns out to be wrong, not much is lost except a bit of time wasted on prayer and piety. I don't know if being an agnostic disqualifies me from making a judgment on this, but Pascal's wager does not sound to me like a very spiritual approach to the realm of the divine.

At another point in his *Pensées*, Pascal writes, "If I saw no signs of a divinity, I would fix myself in denial. If I saw everywhere the marks of a Creator, I would repose peacefully in faith. But seeing too much to deny [Him], and too little to assure me, I am in a pitiful state, and I would wish a hundred times that if a God sustains nature it would reveal Him without ambiguity."

As someone who is still grappling with this faith business and hoping for the best, I can relate. But again, this *pensée* sounds more like a man struggling with his agnosticism than a religious apologist.

Yet in the end, not only did Pascal believe in God, he also believed in the revelations of the Scriptures. And I think the basis of that faith was his astonishment at finding himself *arbitrarily* existing at a particular time in a particular place. Maybe this arbitrariness does not imply that life is purposeless, after all; maybe it suggests that an individual life is some kind of miracle.

Pascal said that being "engulfed in the infinite immensity of spaces of which I am ignorant" both frightens and astonishes him. It is that "astonished" part that gets to me. That I just happen to be in this particular place at this particular historical moment astonishes me for the *very reason* that it is arbitrary. In an arbitrary cosmos, I could just as easily exist at another time and/or in a different place—in fact, in an infinite number of alternative times and places. Or, for that matter, in *no time or place at all.* But this just happens to be it—my personal time and place. Indeed, sometimes my existence here and now does feel like a miracle. Certainly Pascal would agree that the odds were against it.

I believe most of us have had moments when, from out of the blue, we suddenly marvel at the singular fact that we exist right now. How amazing: *I am right here right now!*

Such moments are fleeting and rare, but they often remain with us. A poignant description of that feeling can be found in the ballad "Listen Here," by that quirky jazz genius Dave Frishberg:

When you're still, do you hear
One small voice crystal clear,
Saying "Listen here, my friend, listen here"?
Well, that voice is your own, and it speaks to you alone.
"You can count on me," it says.
"So listen here."
This is you, this is real
This is truly the way you feel . . .

Thank you for that, Mr. Frishberg.

"You are made of stuff that is as old as the planet,
one third as old as the universe, though this is the first
time that those atoms have been gathered together
such that they think that they are you."

....

—FRANK CLOSE, BRITISH PARTICLE PHYSICIST
(1945–), MONIST/MATERIALIST

I READ THIS LINE RECENTLY IN FRANK CLOSE'S *PARTICLE PHYSICS: A Very Short Introduction*, and it bopped me in the head with something that felt very much like spiritual wonder.

That is paradoxical, because Close's statement is clearly as materialist as you can get. For him, as for most physicists, material (fundamentally atoms and their inner structures) is all there is, nothing more and nothing less. No realm of the immaterial exists in such a worldview, no gods or souls or independent minds that are not reducible to atomic activity. And don't even start thinking about free will—everything we do is determined by atoms bouncing around this way and that.

So what is it that bopped me on the spiritual side of my head?

It is the *permanence* of everything in the universe. All the basic stuff has been here since the Big Bang and will remain here for as long as there is Time. What we think of as the development of the universe or, on a far smaller scale, the history and evolution of human beings on this particular planet, is only the endless assembling and reassembling of this same stuff in different combinations at different points in time. This strikes what I may mistakenly think of as my mind with wonder.

I take some kind of sublime comfort in being part of this permanence. Something primal in me rejoices in this connection to Eternity. I realize, of course, that when my particular combination of atoms dismantles (some call it "dying"), my disassembled atoms will have no consciousness of ever having been me. Nonetheless, the fact that the far-flung atoms that were once combined as "me" will remain out there eternally provides me with some contentment. Being a member in good standing of the community of atoms may be this materialist's way of getting inside the Eastern spiritual idea of "being one with everything."

Okay, I do have to admit that this idea of endlessly combining and recombining atoms also gives me the infantile hope that someday those high-flying atoms will gather together as me once more—you know, just for laughs. After all, there is an awful lot of Time out there in Eternity for this particular atomic combo to make an encore. In fact, maybe those atoms have already combined as me at some other time, perhaps in some other galaxy. I try not to get too carried away with this scenario, though; it can feel more like playing a video game in my head than a spiritual experience.

But while I am being fanciful, I will allow myself one more whimsical speculation. Frank Close and other theoretical physicists talk about the possibility of the existence of dimensions other than the three spatial dimensions and one temporal dimension that we know. The reason they entertain this possibility is that there are newly discovered phenomena that they otherwise cannot account for. Recently, physicists at Fermilab detected a puzzling characteristic of subatomic particles called neutrinos—particles that have no charge and barely any mass. Under certain conditions, a high number of these particles transform into charged electron neutrinos. Thus far, no one has been able to come up with a reasonable explanation for what they call this "low-energy excess." So now these scientists are speculating about a new kind of neutrino that, as they say, "may be bouncing in and out of extra dimensions."

To be honest, I cannot begin to grasp what these physicists at Fermilab do in there, let alone what is puzzling them, and I certainly cannot imagine what an "extra dimension" would be. But I do marvel at the fact that they think such dimensions might exist and that their reason for thinking so is that otherwise they cannot make head or tail out of these newly discovered particles. Well, who knows what might be going on in that extra dimension? Maybe—*here's where I take my whimsical leap*—maybe out there in an extra dimension they just might come across a Divine Being. Hey, they may even come across A. J. Ayer having a heart-to-heart with Him. I *said* I was taking a whimsical leap.

As I take my leave of those fellows at Fermilab, I am reminded of the extra dimension I puzzled over when I was a little kid. When my Polish-born, Yiddish-speaking grandmother visited us, she often made mention of the "Needles Dimension." I remember trying to imagine what this dimension looked like—a spherical pincushion? My puzzlement ended when my brother informed me that Grandma, in her thick accent, was saying, "*Needless to mention.*"

Okay, one last bit of whimsy here, this one totally irrelevant to Frank Close's quote, but nonetheless irresistible: A stunning characteristic of some of these newly discovered neutrinos is that they move faster than the speed of light. No sooner was this phenomenon announced in the physics journals than a brand-new joke started circulating on wonky websites:

First line: "We don't allow faster-than-light neutrinos in here," said the bartender.
Second line: A neutrino walks into a bar.

The gag turns on Albert Einstein's conception that if something travels faster than light, it travels backward in time.

Forgive me this irrelevant gag. It's those bouncing atoms that made me tell it.

> "Death is not an event in life: we do not live to experience death. If we take eternity to mean not infinite temporal duration but timelessness, then eternal life belongs to those who live in the present. Our life has no end in the way in which our visual field has no limits."
>
> ....
>
> —LUDWIG WITTGENSTEIN, AUSTRIAN-BRITISH PHILOSOPHER
> (1889–1951), ANALYTIC PHILOSOPHER

I WONDER IF I HAVE A PROBLEM. I DEFINITELY HAVE A TENDENCY to seek spiritual inspiration from super-rational thinkers rather than from rabbis and priests and theologians. Traveling this route may only get me halfway up to the spiritual world.

Ludwig Wittgenstein, generally considered the greatest philosopher of the twentieth century, did not need an extra dimension to dazzle me. He took that old standby dimension, Time, and deconstructed it in a way that threatens to permanently rewire my brain—that is, if I could completely understand him.

It is a comfort to know that I am not alone in having trouble wrapping my mind around many of Wittgenstein's pronouncements. A Cambridge University legend has it that after Wittgenstein had defended his Ph.D. thesis before a panel that included the distinguished philosophers Bertrand Russell and G. E. Moore, Wittgenstein strolled up to them and said, "Don't worry. I know you'll never understand it." Wittgenstein's thesis, by the way, was his ground-breaking essay on the logic of language called the *Tractatus Logico-Philosophicus.*

Understand him or not, just about everyone who has dipped into Wittgenstein's work has been spellbound by it. In seemingly simple statements, he takes our preconceived ideas and makes them do triple flips right before our eyes.

The first part of Wittgenstein's Eternity argument is not hard to grasp. Most of us agree that we will not experience being dead because there will be nobody at home to have that experience. Epicurus said something similar when he wrote, "Death is nothing to us, since when we are, death has not come, and when death has come, we are not."

Both philosophers appear to take some solace in that fact, although many others point out that what strikes terror in their hearts is knowing *now* that in the future they will no longer be.

It is in Wittgenstein's next phrase, "If we take eternity to mean not infinite temporal duration but timelessness," where things start to get tricky. Most of us feel we have a grasp of "infinite temporal duration." It is time that just keeps going on endlessly. It is an infinite number of minutes, an infinite number of Tuesdays, an infinite number of decades. But it is along about here where we may stumble, because an infinite number of minutes is the *same length* as an infinite number of Tuesdays and as an infinite number of decades. They measure out the same; they are all of infinite length. Well, that is not quite right, because infinite durations cannot be measured in the same way we usually measure minutes and Tuesdays and decades; that is, we cannot measure them in a finite context the way we would when counting out, say, five trillion Tuesdays. That is a whole lot of Tuesdays, but they are still measurable. Because we cannot measure an infinite number of Tuesdays in the same way, it seems safe to say that they are immeasurable. It is here where we get a sense of Wittgenstein's notion that "infinite temporal duration" means "timelessness." If it is immeasurable, it is no longer in Time as we conceive it. So we can regard it as timeless.

But then we get to the conclusion of Wittgenstein's proposition: "then eternal life belongs to those who live in the present." *Huh?* That seems like quite a leap—almost immeasurable, so to speak. Is the legendary word analyst just playing with words? We get how "eternity" means "timelessness," but how did we get from "timelessness" to "eternal life in the here and now"?

A number of philosophers have plausibly argued that ultimately the past exists only in a mental construct we call memory. The future exists only as a mental construct, too; it is something we imagine or project based on our experience that because things kept going on and on in the past—one thing after another—they will keep going on that way in the future. In both cases, these mental activities are happening *in the present.* So all we ultimately have is the present—the here and now.

But how did we get from here and now to Eternity? In Wittgenstein's way of thinking, it is because the present is all there is. It is *always* the present. Like right now, for example. And now. Thus, all we really have is the Eternal Now. This I can grasp—most of the time.

But here is where I run into a different kind of problem. When Wittgenstein says that "eternal life belongs to those who live in the present," he is suggesting that this kind of eternal life is available only to certain people and not to others. Living in the present is not merely the nature of the universal human condition, we have to actually *do* something to be there. It takes some doing for the Eternal Now to "belong" to us. And that is that we need to be here now *totally.*

That doesn't sound like a logical inference to me; it sounds like existential guidance. It sounds a little bit like Zen Buddhism via Baba Ram Dass: "Be Here Now." It even sounds somewhat Christian—we do not get Eternal life unless we are fully receptive to it.

That is the part of Wittgenstein's proposition that turns my mind to religion, this implication that there is something virtually holy about fully living in the present, that at those moments when we do so perfectly we can participate in Eternity. Many religious thinkers urge us to find holiness in ordinary experiences, but Wittgenstein's idea goes beyond this. He is saying that *any* experience— ordinary or extraordinary—can become sublime *if we are wholly conscious of it, wholly alive to it.* Then we have the extraordinary opportunity to participate in the Eternal Now.

The celebrated logician Rudolf Carnap, who claimed that Wittgenstein was his greatest inspiration, once wrote: "[Wittgenstein's] point of view and his attitude toward people and problems, even theoretical problems, were much more similar to those of a creative artist than to those of a scientist; one might almost say, similar to those of a religious prophet or a seer. . . . When finally, sometimes after a prolonged arduous effort, his answers came forth, his statement stood before us like a newly created piece of art or a divine revelation . . . the impression he made on us was as if insight came to him as through divine inspiration, so that we could not help feeling that any sober rational comment of analysis of it would be a profanation."

Amen.

> "Live as if you were living a second time, and as though
> you had acted wrongly the first time."
>
> ....
>
> —VIKTOR FRANKL, AUSTRIAN NEUROLOGIST, PSYCHIATRIST,
> AND PHILOSOPHER (1905–1997), EXISTENTIALIST PSYCHOLOGIST

HERE WE HAVE A PITHY MAXIM THAT IS A PHILOSOPHICAL THOUGHT experiment in itself. But before embarking on that experiment, it is important to know some essential facts about its author.

Viktor Frankl came to Existentialist philosophy as a result of unique and horrifying experiences: He was a prisoner in Nazi concentration camps for four years. He was a slave laborer during some of that period. He lost his wife and parents to the Holocaust.

After being liberated by American troops in 1945, Frankl returned to Vienna, where he resumed his neurological and psychiatric practice. In that same year, he wrote an account of how his camp experiences shaped his philosophy and his radically new approach to psychotherapy. Its German title, literally translated, is *Nevertheless, Say "Yes" to Life: A Psychologist Experiences the Concentration Camp.* More than ten years later, the book was published in America with the title *Man's Search for Meaning.* Since that time, it has become a classic of Existentialist writing.

The "Nevertheless" of his title refers to the daily horrors of life in the concentration camps. In spite of enduring those horrors, Frankl maintains that a person still possessed the freedom to choose a meaning for his life—a reason to remain alive—and that finding meaning answers man's most basic drive.

Unlike Sigmund Freud, who posited the sex drive as fundamental, and Alfred Adler, who saw the will to power as the prime motive, Frankl deemed that the need for "logos"—Greek for "meaning" or "rational principle"—supersedes all other drives. When a man is stripped of everything—his health, his safety, his dignity, his hope for rescue—he is still left with the capacity to fulfill his yearning for meaning. Indeed, he can still affirm his life, say "Yes" to it.

Writes Frankl, "Every day, every hour, offered the opportunity to make a decision, a decision which determined whether you would or would not submit to those powers which threatened to rob you of your very self, your inner freedom; which determined whether or not you would become the plaything of circumstance, renouncing freedom and dignity to become molded into the form of the typical inmate."

Frankl's resulting form of Existential therapy, "logotherapy," became known as the Third Viennese School of psychotherapy. A basic tenet of this therapy is that even when we think we have lost all control over our lives, as a prisoner does in the extreme, we may yet control our *attitude* toward life. We may find meaning in our bare existence. That is one freedom of which no one can rob us.

Frankl's philosophy and innovative therapy methods put his critics in a difficult position. How could anyone publicly find fault with anything that had been created out of the horrific experiences Frankl had endured? Yet, years after the book's publication, some critics dared to say that they found Frankl simplistic, more like a pop, feel-good guru than a serious theoretician. Frankl was even compared to Reverend Norman Vincent Peale, the 1950s mass market purveyor of "The Power of Positive Thinking." For example, some were convinced Frankl had gone off the deep end when he stated, apparently in all seriousness, "I recommend that the Statue of Liberty on the East Coast be supplemented by a Statue of Responsibility on the West Coast."

I do have to admit that one sounds more like something a Boy Scout leader might say than a founder of the Third Viennese School of Psychotherapy. But that said, I actually do find something worthwhile in positive thinking, especially in today's climate of nonstop irony and cynicism. I am not talking smiley-face Pollyannaism, but a simple, "Nevertheless, Yes" seems like a better option than cynicism if I have the choice—and I do believe I have that choice.

Simple thoughts need not be simplistic. Just because Grandma's adages sound hackneyed doesn't mean they are without value. Here and there, Oprah issues a homily that is worthy of our consideration. There is a plain and simple passage in Thornton Wilder's timeless play *Our Town* that still haunts and inspires me. It deeply expresses both the sublimity of fully appreciating life and the difficulty of doing so. In the play, Emily, now deceased, invisibly revisits her hometown, and is saddened by her loved ones' lack of consciousness of their lives:

Emily: *Does anyone ever realize life while they live it . . .*
   every, every minute?
Replies the Stage Manager (a character in the play):
   No. Saints and poets maybe . . . they do some.

When Frankl says that finding a meaning of life naturally implies finding something to feel positive about, he is on to something basic and simple. Actually, it goes both ways: Finding something to feel positive about gives life meaning.

From the time I read *Man's Search for Meaning* soon after it came out in the early 1960s, I was intrigued by Frankl's exercise of deeply imagining the outcome of adopting a particular meaning of life. How would it play out? How would it make me feel? Could this meaning still work for me if I were presented with the worst imaginable obstacles? Into my "Pithies" notebook it went.

This immersion in imaginary outcomes would undoubtedly resonate with Epicurus, the original "outcomes" champion, although, of course, the Greek philosopher had already established the meaning of life—to enjoy it. Which brings me back to Frankl's fascinating existential exercise: "Live as if you were living a second time, and as though you had acted wrongly the first time."

The first part, living a second time, is within the scope of our imaginations, at least as a general idea. We would simply start over again as youngsters—same parents, same town, but basically everything that followed would be up for grabs. Even the idea of making different choices this time around is fairly easy to imagine. Who hasn't fantasized about how their life would have been if she had married Harry instead of Phil? But it is that "as though I had acted *wrongly* the first time" part that puzzles me. It presupposes that I already know what the wrong way to live is. But I don't: If I don't know the right way—and that is why I am trying this exercise in the first place—how can I know what's the wrong way?

The second time around, I understood what Frankl is up to. He is using this exercise as a *strategy* for finding the right way to live. He is making the question of life's purpose into a concrete thought experiment instead of an abstract contemplation. This is not a bad idea considering that any answer to this question is more likely to be found in the realm of imagination than in that of pure intellect. The human mind—at least mine—tends to work from the concrete to the abstract, from personal experiences to principles suggested by these experiences. I am pretty sure that if I sat in the lotus position for days on end on some remote mountaintop and tried to come up with a meaning of life, my mind would soon turn toward something concrete, like the rumblings in my stomach. I would probably then declare that life is a fudge sundae.

But with Frankl's thought experiment, I sit down with a concrete story—the life that, for the sake of the experiment, I am temporarily presupposing is the "wrong" one. He has given me a tool for revving up my imagination, for getting me to dream up a better way to live.

> "The unexamined life is surely worth living, but is
> the unlived life worth examining?"
>
> ....
>
> —ADAM PHILLIPS, BRITISH PSYCHOANALYST AND PHILOSOPHER
> (1954–), FREUDIAN EXISTENTIALIST

OOPS, MAYBE VIKTOR FRANKL'S THOUGHT EXPERIMENT IS NOT such a good idea after all. In fact, maybe the whole enterprise of imagining alternative lives is a prescription for a life of despair.

Once again I find myself discombobulated by a brainy, and counterintuitive, contemporary British thinker. And once again I am heartened to see modern philosophy—especially when it is coupled with psychology—addressing issues of how to live.

In his book *Missing Out: In Praise of the Unlived Life*, the contemporary psychoanalytic writer and philosopher Adam Phillips argues that modern man is so preoccupied with the lives he has not lived that he misses out on appreciating the one life he actually has. This is yet another example of our uncanny predilection for avoiding living in the present. In addition to drifting away from the here-and-now by fantasizing "What next?" we drift off into "What might have been?"

Drawing on his experiences with patients, Phillips concludes that "We think we know more about the experiences we don't have than the experiences we do have." This "unlived life" of our imaginations becomes more vivid and significant than the life we are living. "And what was not possible becomes the story of our lives. . . . Our lives become a protracted mourning for, an endless trauma about, the lives we were unable to live."

I am afraid I know too well what Phillips is talking about. "What if?" scenarios play in my mind regularly: *What if I had moved into Timothy Leary's commune in Millbrook, New York, instead of just nervously pacing past the gates, daring myself to go in? And, What if I had remained on the Greek island of Hydra instead of taking that TV job back in New York?*

Playing the "What ifs?" is not a gratifying way to live. And it is definitely not a way in which to have a positive attitude toward the life we now have and have lived. It is the exact opposite of a life of gratitude for simply being alive.

I have to wonder if all those deep thinkers—from Epicurus to Frankl—who urge us to calculate the outcomes of various imagined courses of action are innocently sending us out on a self-destructive mission. *"Live as if you were living a second time"?* Hey, how about living as though you are living for the *first* and *last* time? From Phillips's point of view, the latter is the way the richest life is lived.

Which brings me back to Phillips's flippant flip of Socrates's famous "unexamined life" line ("The unexamined life is not worth living"). Phillips is calling into question the fundamental methodology of traditional psychotherapy and the entire "self-actualization" movement. Here is how Phillips puts it: "I don't want to say self-knowledge is useless. But we need to know when self-knowledge is genuinely useful and when it isn't. There are some situations where the struggle to 'know' *about* an experience is a distraction from the experience itself."

Like many people in my generation, I engaged in psychotherapy from time to time in my twenties and thirties. Part of my motive, of course, was to feel better about myself and life in general, but there was another incentive that was very much in the air in those days: to learn in depth who I was. It seemed like a natural extension of the ideas of examining life and being true to one's self. Psychotherapy was the logical next step in a diligent student's education.

In this process, most of us "discovered" that Mom and Dad had burdened us with any number of neurotic habits and compulsions. We dredged up scenes of our childhood when we believed we were belittled and emotionally wounded. As a result, of course, we got angry at our parents. The twentieth-century British poet Philip Larkin provided us with a catchy theme song for our plight in his popular poem "This Be The Verse":

> *They fuck you up, your mum and dad.*
> *They may not mean to, but they do.*
> *They fill you with the faults they had*
> *And add some extra, just for you.*

Being resentful of our upbringings often had the effect of replacing our malaise with anger, not altogether an improvement. We were still stuck in distressed emotions. And from Adam Phillips's point of view, we were still filtering our experiences through a screen of self-knowledge.

Psychotherapists would say that this business of identifying the source of our unwelcome habits and feelings is only one step in the process of becoming psychologically liberated from them. After his last session, the successful patient leaves his shrink's office both wise and autonomous, having finally let go of his anger and ready to move on. Would that it always played out as neatly as that.

In any event, Phillips has my number. I continue to keep lugging around bagsful of self-knowledge, most of it trivial and much of it of dubious veracity.

I can't help wondering if I wouldn't be feeling better about myself if I had never read *Missing Out*.

> "If you believe that feeling bad or worrying long enough
> will change a past or future event, then you are residing
> on another planet with a different reality system."
>
> ....
>
> —WILLIAM JAMES, AMERICAN PHILOSOPHER
> (1842–1910), CLASSICAL PRAGMATIST

I HAVE ALWAYS FOUND IT HARD TO RESIST PROFESSOR JAMES'S advice. For starters, it is often witty, like his "residing on another planet" bit. It is also folksy and sensible, at times just good old-fashioned common sense. (James once wrote that "[c]ommon sense and a sense of humor are the same thing, moving at different speeds. A sense of humor is just common sense, dancing.")

Basically, he is urging us to stop worrying, because it has no good outcome, in fact, not much of an outcome at all except wasted time. Oprah says stuff like that, too, and I would be hard pressed to argue this idea with either James or Winfrey.

But I have had a problem with it ever since I copied this quote into my notebook at the age of twenty. I definitely do not believe that feeling bad or worrying long is good for the soul—or for the digestion either, for that matter. But whether I believe in it or not, getting myself to stop feeling bad and to stop worrying is another predicament altogether.

Feeling bad has a life of its own, totally apart from our beliefs about its value. That is why man invented bourbon and Prozac. William James of all people understood that: He suffered from periodic bouts of intractable depression. Furthermore, he was the philosopher who said that inebriation was a way to say "Yes" to the cosmos, while sobriety produced a resounding "No." So perhaps he was ultimately saying in his epigram: "Do whatever it takes to stop feeling bad, including downing a couple of shots of bourbon."

That said, recently I have had to own up to the fact that I actually do have more direct control over my moods and my worrying than I used to believe I had, and not just through chemical assistance. For a long time, I had been caught up in the psychoanalytic idea that we are slaves to our feelings and only by digging long and deep into our psyches can we gain any control over them. Although most of us have never studied Freud's theories in depth, his basic conceptions of the psyche and its development permeate our culture. We uncritically accept his ideas of unconscious motivations and unruly neuroses; that is why we are convinced that most of our feelings and moods are beyond our conscious control.

But lately that way of thinking strikes me as a bit of a cop-out, a way of not taking responsibility for how I feel. It is the contemporary variation on the old alibi, "The devil made me do it"—"My unconscious made me *feel* it."

It took marrying a Dutch Calvinist for me to reconsider my

attitude. When I worry obsessively about something, Freke often says, "Stop doing that!" or words to that effect. Said with a Dutch accent, this gets one's attention. Freke is more of the pull-yourself-up-by-your-bootstraps school than the analyze-your-inner-drives school when it comes to moods and worries. She believes not only in a free will but in a strong one. So over the years, I have had to grudgingly admit that there is something to be said for my wife's school of direct conscious responsibility for our feelings. I just wish it wasn't so hard to do.

One last thought about James's advice by way of the sixteenth-century French philosopher Michel de Montaigne. He once quipped, "My life has been full of terrible misfortunes most of which never happened."

There go about half the things I feel bad about.

> "Do every act of your life as though it were
> the very last act of your life."
>
> ....
>
> —MARCUS AURELIUS, ROMAN EMPEROR AND PHILOSOPHER
> (AD 121–180), STOIC

DEFINITELY A KEEPER. IF THERE IS ANY SINGLE LESSON I WANT TO carry with me to my final day, this one's it.

If Marcus Aurelius's declaration has a familiar ring, it is because philosophers and religious thinkers have been saying more or less the same thing from time immemorial.

Be here now.

Be ever mindful.

Live in the present.

From modern philosophers, one of the clearest and most forceful iterations of this sentiment comes from Henry David Thoreau: "You must live in the present, launch yourself on every wave, find your eternity in each moment. Fools stand on their island of opportunities and look toward another land. There is no other land; there is no other life but this."

Clearly, we human beings must have great difficulty living

mindfully in the present, otherwise why would so many philosophers feel the need to keep repeating the message?

On the face of it, fully engaging in the here and now does not sound that difficult. *Here* is right here in front of us. And it is *now* right now. So what's the problem?

Some people drift away from the present by desiring something better than what exists here and now. Others, like me, drift away into "What's next?" Another, more thoroughgoing way of avoiding full immersion in the present is by seeing all of life as stages of preparation, ranging from preparing for dinner to preparing for life in the Hereafter, with preparing for final exams falling somewhere in between. At the other extreme, there are those of us who persistently dwell in the past, with either nostalgia or regret or a mix of the two.

This drifting away from the present comes along with the human capacities of imagination and extended memory. We can always imagine our lives as different from what they actually are; we can always see alternatives. Apparently, that is a temptation that is hard for most of us to resist. Likewise, we can remember the way life was in the past, and chewing that over also seems irresistible.

Of course, a life with no anticipation of the future has serious drawbacks. For example, when we get hungry around dinnertime, there may be nothing in the pantry if we have not planned and executed shopping. Left to his own devices, Snookers, who never planned a moment of his life, would be seriously hungry much of the day. (As part of our deal, I plan and execute his dinners.) Yet

Snookers, presumably without the capacities to either plan or regret, has the gift of always living in the present. And judging by the cues available—the sparkle in his eyes, the wag of his tail—he finds almost every present moment absolutely dandy.

The planning we humans do often takes up the bulk of our consciousness, particularly with our propensity for endlessly reviewing our plans like a looped soundtrack in our minds. I know many people who make detailed lists of what they hope to accomplish on a given day. Some tell me that they take great pleasure in checking off items once they are done. It sometimes sounds like this "checking-off" pleasure is greater than the doing itself.

I suspect that there is something about living fully in the present that deeply frightens us. This dread might be right up there with Freud's basic drive, the libido, as a basic condition of being human. Indeed, those two conditions appear to complement each other: sex is one of the few dependable times when we are firmly engaged in the here and now.

But what could be the source of our fear of living in the present? One reason could be that we live in perpetual terror of being disappointed by our lives, indeed, by life itself. We know intuitively that life in the here and now is life's ultimate—life cannot get any realer than *right now*. But what if we find the here-and-now life seriously lacking? What if it strikes us with the full force of "Is that all there is?" What if we find this ultimate reality uninspiring or, worse, hard, unfair, and painful? To deal with this fear of existential disappointment we make a preemptive strike on living in the present by reflexively imagining something different, by switching our consciousness to the future or past or to an imagined alternative life.

Another possible reason we refrain from living in the present is that it is fraught with intimations of our mortality. When we are fully immersed in the here and now, we become profoundly aware of the unstoppable progression of time and change. Most of us have experienced highly charged moments of bliss occasioned by simple events—a sudden appearance of a flock of doves overhead; an astonishing performance of a passage of music; an enchanting smile on the face of a passing stranger. These moments are fleeting. That is an essential part of their intensity. But these fleeting moments leave us with a bittersweet awareness that everything ends. And with that awareness comes the inescapable knowledge of our personal finitude. We are fully cognizant of the fact that the sum of our here-and-now moments will reach their end and then we will be no more.

Again, there is a connection between sex and the hyperawareness of death we experience when we are totally present. The French language refers to *la petite mort* ("the little death") that many people experience immediately following orgasm. The term refers to a feeling of deep melancholy that sometimes follows this intense engagement with one of life's most powerful forces. Climax, then nothingness. This "little death" carries with it a presentiment of the big one.

This phenomenon goes in the opposite direction, too. As much as we fear inhabiting the here and now, we deeply yearn to be as fully alive as possible. And one way we pursue the goal of feeling intensely alive is by tempting death. We jump off cliffs to go hang gliding; we race cars at dangerous speeds; some apparently even indulge in the extreme sport of volcano surfing in which the death defier sails around the rim of volcano on what is called an ash board. The payoff of these mortal risks is that they rivet us to the here and now. Facing death, we become supremely alive. Many Existentialist thinkers believe that squarely facing our mortality is the only sure way to become fully alive in the present, although I am pretty sure that Jean-Paul Sartre, with his thick glasses and frail physique, did not have volcano surfing in mind.

Now you tell me!

This is the one that prompted me to close the book on "Pithies" in my midthirties. The whole enterprise struck me as naïve and futile. Enough already.

But some forty years later, here I am again, fascinated by these philosophers' ideas about how to live. And now, thinking again about Niebuhr's quote, I am more perplexed by it than ever—which was probably Professor Niebuhr's intent.

Like his mentor, the theologian Paul Tillich, Niebuhr analyzed man's predicament in Existentialist terms. A basic question both men asked was, Why can't man rid himself of sin if he has the radical freedom to create himself and his values?

The answer, Niebuhr said, is that even as man contemplates the divine, he remains stuck with a finite mind that can never get a comprehensive bead on transcendent values. A perfect understanding of sin is ultimately beyond us. We cannot climb out of this existential duality; we possess the ability to ponder our mortality, good and evil, and the "meaning of life," but we are unable to ever really see the Big Picture. We just don't have the equipment for it.

Often, Niebuhr displayed a sense of humor about what he saw as man's predicament. He concluded one sermon by saying, "What a contradiction—to be the judge of all things and yet to be a worm of the earth." Not exactly a thigh-slapper, but not bad for a sermon.

Niebuhr was also concerned with man's place in the immanent world, the world of cultures and societies and political creeds. After the rise of Nazism, he began to focus on the "herd mentality" that Nietzsche had so abhorred. Niebuhr brooded over man's weakness in the face of conformist human behavior. Also like Nietzsche, he believed that as long as we remain a product of our culture, we cannot rise above its values.

I think this is what was on Niebuhr's mind when he quipped, "Every time I find the meaning of life, they change it." Like political creeds and advertising slogans, philosophies of life arise and fall in a culture. When I look back at the early entries in my "Pithies" notebook, I realize how much I had been influenced by the popularity of the philosophies of the 1960s and 1970s, how uncritically I accepted the social nihilism and self-centeredness of Aldous Huxley and Timothy Leary along with the ennui and melancholia of Albert Camus and Jean-Paul Sartre. In doing so, I was undoubtedly indulging in some herd mentality. Still, these thinkers *did* help me to see philosophy as a way to thoughtfully inform my life.

Right about now I can hear Adam Phillips admonishing me to stop thinking about my past and all the what-if scenarios that come along with it. So suffice it to say that Niebuhr's point is well taken: Any minute now they are going to change the meaning of life. Again.

Caveat emptor!

Epilogue

FIGURE OUT THE MEANING OF LIFE? WHO AM I KIDDING? WHO DO I think I am?

Actually, after reading what Derek Parfit has to say about degrees of personal identity, "Who do I think I am?" is a pretty intriguing question. Could there be different meanings of life depending on what self I happen to be at any given moment?

Right there, in asking that question, is my problem in a nutshell. I am fascinated by the questions philosophers raise and the answers to these questions that they offer. They bewitch me. But at the same time, I am skeptical of any philosopher who thinks he knows any absolute answer. I gather that this sequence—*question, answer, skeptical response to the answer . . . next question, please*—is what professional philosophers do full time. It is like taking a hair-raising spin in a racing car only to discover that the roadway is a Mobius strip. But what can I say? I never seem to tire of the ride.

This is why that Bertrand Russell quote I jotted down resonates with me. I still take great pleasure in playing around with philosophical questions, the ones that Russell is the first to admit have no unequivocal answers. (Indeed, Russell says that is exactly what makes them philosophical questions and not scientific problems.) I guess this quality makes me a Cerebral Hedonist, although some would say it makes me a mental masochist. I imagine if I had taken different roads along the way, I would have found my greatest pleasure in fly fishing or playing the banjo. I certainly do not believe for a minute that my form of hedonism is better than any other—at least as long as that hedonism does not hurt any innocent bystanders.

One thing that struck me as I went over my collection of aphorisms and quotes is how often the paramount value of fully engaging in the present crops up and the various routes different philosophers take to arrive at this value. Epicurus makes it a centerpiece of his philosophy by counseling us to cease from always wanting something more than or different from what we have right now. Marcus Aurelius hits this idea even more forcefully by advising us to act as if every action were our last. Millennia later, Henry David Thoreau articulates it with both simplicity and passion in his admonition to "launch yourself on every wave." And the idea is catapulted into the transcendental realm in Wittgenstein's breathtaking declaration, "[E]ternal life belongs to those who live in the present."

Of course, the main reason the "Be here now" dictum keeps popping up in this collection is that I am this collection's collector and I have always been drawn to this idea. Yet it took reviewing the various expressions of this idea for me to think more thoroughly about why fully living in the present is so hard to do—at least, for me.

Which brings me back to the various brands of hedonism. There is nothing like engaging in an activity that yields great pleasure to bring a person fully into the here and now. In fact, it is a twofer—the activity produces pleasure in itself *and* that pleasure is multiplied by its putting us in that delightful space of the here and now. Playing a good game of tennis can do that for some people. Making a soufflé can do it for others. Sex can do it for most everyone. And for some people, frolicking around with philosophical questions does the trick.

Being a hedonist of any stripe is a choice we have. But making that choice often involves challenging the rules and customs of our culture, tribe, religion, and family. We do not need to opt for the wild and bawdy hedonism of an Aristippus to come up against "inherited truths" that stand between us and our fondest pleasure. Simply deciding, after an expensive college education, that our greatest pleasure would be to work on an organic farm can be a formidable challenge. Nietzsche sees meeting this challenge, whatever it may be, as necessary to becoming fully human.

I am more convinced than ever that each individual has the capacity to consciously choose his own reason for living, whether that means becoming a committed Episcopalian, a Freedom Fighter, or a beach bum—or possibly all three. I also believe that deliberately choosing that meaning and then owning it makes our lives richer—more "authentic," as Sartre would say—than if we simply let our lives happen. I guess that makes me a bona fide Existentialist.

Still, I feel more than a little foolish about offering even this bit of advice on how to live. Binx Bolling, in my favorite passage of Walker Percy's *The Moviegoer*, has the final word on folks who propound life credos:

> *I listen every night at ten to a program called This I Believe. . . . On the program hundreds of the highest-minded people in our country, thoughtful and intelligent people, people with mature inquiring minds, state their personal credos. The two or three hundred I have heard so far were without exception admirable people. . . . If I had to name a single trait that all these people shared, it is their niceness. Their lives are triumphs of niceness. They like everyone with the warmest and most generous feelings. And as for themselves: it would be impossible for even a dour person not to like them.*
>
> *Tonight's subject is a playwright who transmits this very quality of niceness in his plays. He begins:*
> *"I believe in people. I believe in tolerance and understanding between people. I believe in the uniqueness and the dignity of the individual—"*

Everyone on This I Believe believes in the uniqueness and dignity of the individual. I have noticed, however, that the believers are hardly unique themselves, are in fact like peas in a pod.

Guilty as charged, Binx. But I do have to say, it is kind of comfy here in the pod.

Afterword

ONE OF MY GREATEST PLEASURES IN HAVING A BOOK PUBLISHED IS that I hear from readers. They write to me from all over the world with ideas and experiences of their own and, when I am really lucky, with jokes I have never heard. All of which makes me happy—even when a letter accuses me of having made a dumb mistake. Indeed, I am happy even when they are right. (I like to attribute this to my late-in-life new-found maturity, although my wife believes it's simply because I enjoy attention any way I can get it.)

In response to this book, I have received a great number of letters that contain the correspondents' own favorite pithies and why these pithies resonate with them. To my surprise, a good number of these letters and accompanying pithies were about dogs—what these four-footed friends mean to them and, particularly, what these people learn from them. I know I used my late, sweet companion, Snookers, as an example in parts of this book, but I hadn't realized he had made that great an impression.

I am pleased to report that the two most-sent dog pithies originated with two of my favorite ancient Greek philosophers, Diogenes and Plato.

> *"Dogs and philosophers do the greatest good and get the fewest rewards."*
>
> —*Diogenes*

And,

> *"Your dog is a true philosopher."*
>
> —*Plato*

Diogenes of Sinope, also known as Diogenes the Cynic, is popularly remembered for his prank of carrying around a lantern in daylight, saying that he was searching for an honest man. I use the word "prank" advisedly. Diogenes apparently loved to play the public fool around the Athens of his time (the 300s BCE). A homeless beggar who often slept, doglike, in an outdoor clay crock, he firmly believed that lessons were better taught by actions than by Socratic dialogues and lectures. Thus, his lantern shtick was his satirical way of dramatizing that a truly honest man is hard to find.

His "Dogs and philosophers" quote is doubly self-serving. He clearly considered himself a great and underappreciated philosopher, indeed a far superior philosopher to Plato, who was all about mere words. And in a remarkable number of ways, Diogenes proudly identified with canines. He cursed the people of his culture for living phony, unnatural lives, while praising dogs for doing what comes naturally—for example, peeing in public, eating whatever they came across in the street, and sleeping alfresco. But most significantly to me, Diogenes admired dogs' natural ability to live in the moment without worrying about the past or future. Snookers, my personal Diogenes, certainly impressed me with that particular lesson.

In his own time and culture, Diogenes was considered a nutcase, especially for some of his doglike behavior, like peeing in public, frequently on the sandals of those who disagreed with him. (The label "Cynic" comes directly from the ancient Greek word for "doglike.") No doubt, if he were living today in our culture, he would be carted off to some government-run institution. His preference, I imagine, would be the dog pound.

Happily, Diogenes's unconventional take on the world survived him and he is now considered one of the great Greek philosophers. In his final resting place, Corinth, he is memorialized with a tall pillar on which rests a glorious marble dog.

I have to admit that I glossed over the Plato quote when I first read *The Republic* decades ago, but at that time I wasn't the dog lover and admirer I came to be when I grew older. "Your dog is a true philosopher" appears in the section where Socrates engages Glaucon in a dialogue about the traits that would be required of the Guardians (or Philosopher Kings) to govern the ideal society. I found it enjoyable to reopen my old copy of *The Republic* and trace down this quote that several readers had sent. I had forgotten how entertaining—at times, goofy—the Socratic dialogues can be.

Socrates: Would not he who is fitted to be a guardian, besides the spirited nature, need to have the qualities of a philosopher?

Glaucon: I do not apprehend your meaning.

S: The trait of which I am speaking, I replied, may be also seen in the dog, and is remarkable in the animal.

G: What trait?

S: Why, a dog, whenever he sees a stranger, is angry; when an acquaintance, he welcomes him, although the one has never done him any harm, nor the other any good. Did this never strike you as curious?

G: The matter never struck me before; but I quite recognize the truth of your remark.

S: And surely this instinct of the dog is very charming; —*your dog is a true philosopher.*

G: Why?

S: Why, because he distinguishes the face of a friend and of an enemy only by the criterion of knowing and not knowing. And must not an animal be a lover of learning who determines what he likes and dislikes by the test of knowledge and ignorance?

G: Most assuredly.

S: And is not the love of learning the love of wisdom,
     which is philosophy?

G: They are the same, he replied.

Back in the day when I wrote routines for comedians, working for comedy duos—a Straight Man and a Gagster—were the most coveted gigs because one didn't have to wrestle with the problem of setting up a joke: he could have the Straight Man do it directly. Consider this old vaudeville routine:

Straight Man: Who was that lady I saw you with last
     night?

Gagster: That was no lady, that was my wife.

Undoubtedly, the writer of this routine started out with the idea of calling one's wife something less than a lady. He thought this bit of daring naughtiness would generate laughs. (In that pre–politically correct era, a "lady" possessed "class" while all other women did not.) So the writer made a draft of the punch line first: "She is not a lady, she is my wife." Then all he had to do was set it up with the "Who was that lady . . ." straight line and redraft the punch line accordingly. No problem, since the writer was writing both parts.

I'm pretty sure that is the way Plato wrote his dialogues. He had a point he wanted to make, so he had his straight man—in the previous case, Glaucon—set him up and then agree with just about anything he said. At times, it seems as if Plato could prove almost anything with this method. Consider this exchange:

Socrates: [A dog] distinguishes the face of a friend and of an enemy only by the criterion of knowing and not knowing. And must not an animal be a lover of learning who determines what he likes and dislikes by the test of knowledge and ignorance?

Glaucon: Most assuredly.

How's that again, Socrates? We get the point that a dog distinguishes friend from foe by the instinctive criterion of familiarity. But it's that jump to the dog being a lover of learning that confounds us. It would seem to require the dog to *realize* that he has performed this task by this criterion—to be *conscious* of it.

Wow, look at that—I distinguished friend from foe by the test of familiarity, thinks our doggie. *I just adore learning, don't you?*

Plato simply slipped in the dog's *consciousness* of why he is behaving this way, not to mention his *reflection* that he must then be a "lover of learning"? But, hey, Socrates's straight man, Glaucon, assures us that Socrates is on to something with his "dog = philosopher" notion, so I guess he's right. Right?

Actually, Socrates does raise an interesting question: If I learned philosophical lessons from Snookers—and I did—does not that in itself make him a philosopher? I'm afraid not. I have also learned philosophical lessons by lying on my back on a summer's night staring up at a panoply of stars, but this does not make the stars philosophers. Or does it, Glaucon?

Perhaps what Plato/Socrates is saying is that a dog's direct access to pure instinct offers the best wisdom one can have. After all, elsewhere Plato maintains that all knowledge is innate—inside us from the get-go—and just needs to be revealed, so the dog, operating on pure instinct, is on the fast track to sagaciousness. But I'm still not sure I'd want a dog as my supreme leader. I'm not even sure Diogenes would.

But back to the philosophical lessons I learned from Snookers. Often, fooling around with him, I found myself actually envying his lack of self-consciousness. His spontaneity was pure, uncorrupted by consciousness. In particular, he was not conscious that he was mortal—certainly not in any way resembling the way we humans are. In my "the hell with Existentialism" moods, I think of that ignorance as a blissful blessing.

And there were times when, lying with Snookers on the couch and looking into his warm, expressive brown eyes, I'd find myself thinking that he cannot be simply a machine, a bundle of stimulus-response synaptic paths—a neural robot. Because I see something soulful in his eyes. Of course, my reaction could credibly be just my own stimulus-response synaptic paths doing their thing.

Nonetheless, this convinced me that either Snookers and I both possessed selves/souls of some kind or both of us are neural robots. But I just cannot buy the idea that I have a soul and he doesn't— not when staring into those eyes of his.

And yet there were also times when the thought that we were both just bundles of bouncing atoms was a strange comfort to me. It made his death—and mine—more bearable; it was just physical matter doing its combining and recombining thing, nothing to get upset about. But that said, my love for that doggie felt as real as anything else in my world.

I was seventy-five when Snookers died. I was deeply unhappy. My wife suggested that at this stage of my life, it would be better for me to get another dog sooner rather than later. I resisted for a while; the idea that Snookers could be replaced seemed disrespectful of him, callow even. But after a few months, I yearned to have a dog beside me, so I started looking online for Snookers's successor. I have always gotten "used"—previously owned—dogs. (I refuse to use the term "rescue dogs" unless it means that it is I who is being rescued.) I saw a photo of one who was a few hours away from my home; I went and picked him up. My granddaughter named him Guffy.

Guffy looks a lot like Snookers. Often, I mistakenly call him "Snookers." Guffy does not seem to mind. Over the past two years, he has gradually become more "Guffy" than "Snookers" to me. (I am sure Derek Parfit would understand.) I love Guffy.

As it happened, none of my reader correspondents chose my all-time favorite philosophical quote about dogs. It comes from the philosophical master himself, Groucho Marx:

> *"Outside of a dog, a book is man's best friend. Inside of a dog, it's too dark to read."*

—DMK

Glossary of Terms

I am sure many readers are familiar with the terms defined below, but I offer them here on the chance that after college those terms accidentally got buried under more pressing definitions, like what "hashtag" or "selfie" mean.

Absurdism: The concept that we cannot reconcile our desire to find a meaning of life with the fact that it is rationally impossible to do so. Also, various philosophers' ideas on how to lead an absurdist life. Some people who embrace the absurdist outlook find it hilarious in a bittersweet sort of way.

Ad hominem: An abbreviation for *argumentum ad hominem*, meaning an argument against an idea or statement based on the character of the person who authored it. It is sometimes used to discredit a philosophy of life proclaimed by someone who does not live up to it himself, as in, "He talks the talk, but he doesn't walk the walk, so I'm not listening to his advice."

It is the opposite of an **Appeal to Authority**, which is accepting an idea because someone believed to be credible uttered it, as in, "I personally don't know much about the science of climatology, but I believe global warming is a real threat because 95 percent of respected climatologists say that it is."

Agnosticism: The philosophical position that both the existence and nonexistence of a god are unknowable, in contrast to theism (the belief that a god definitely does exist) and atheism (the belief that no god exists). Typically, agnostics sit on the fence for most of their lives, a position they often find uncomfortable.

Anthropocentrism: The worldview that human beings are the most significant element of the universe, especially as compared to other animals or God. It is considered bad form to advocate this position around your pets or God.

Empiricism: The school of philosophy that maintains that knowledge of the external world (as compared to knowledge of analytic logic and its proper applications) comes only from sensory experience. Seventeenth- and eighteenth-century British Empiricism came in reaction to **rationalism**. Empiricism is a stance in **epistemology**. It is sometimes summed up by the statement, "What you see is *all* you get."

Epistemology: The study of knowledge. It basically asks, What is a rational test for knowability? How can we know for certain what is real? How can we know which propositions are true and which are not? What are basic principles of certainty? Epistemology attempts to lay down the line between knowledge and mere belief. It is one of the main topics of philosophy, along with logic, ethics, and metaphysics.

Existentialism: A school of philosophy that places living, conscious human beings at the center of everything worth thinking about. This school is the opposite of Big Picture philosophies, which focus on the nature of the cosmos, with humans as only minor parts of that picture. Some Existentialists hold that life's meaning is something that only the individual can create and it is incumbent upon him to consciously make this choice of meaning.

Falsifiability: In modern philosophy of science, the dictum that a theory can only be valid if there is some conceivable evidence that could disprove it. Psychological theories often fail the test of falsifiability. For example, no matter what evidence was put before Freud—a patient who avowedly loved his mother, one who hated his mother, and one who said he was indifferent to his mother—the Father of Psychoanalysis claimed his theory of the Oedipus complex held up; each of these patients was simply displaying a different manifestation of the Oedipus complex. In other words, no possible evidence could prove his theory false so, according to the rule of falsifiability, it cannot be proven true. That something is "falsifiable" does not mean that it is false; rather, it means that *if* the statement *were* false, its falsehood could be proven. Tricky.

Hedonism: The theory that pleasure is the sole value in life, so go for it. Likewise, pain makes life less pleasant, so do whatever is necessary to avoid it. In short, if it feels good, it *is* good. There are many philosophical variations of Hedonism, all of them a pleasure to think about.

Humanism: The stance that the good of mankind is of prime importance. In modern times, humanism means that pursuing this good has nothing to do with a god; doing good works for other humans is a value in itself, not the fulfillment of a duty to a god.

Irreducibility and Reducibility: These two terms frequently come up in philosophical arguments about whether consciousness is a different phenomenon from brain activity. Can consciousness be meaningfully reduced to brain activity or is consciousness a thing in itself—irreducible to bouncing atoms inside our noggins?

Law of Noncontradiction: One of the basic laws of logic, this law means that two antithetical propositions cannot both be true at the same time and in the same sense. You cannot logically say "X is a football" and "X is not a football" and claim that both are true at the same time and in the same sense. Without the Law of Noncontradiction, no rational discourse is possible.

Logical Positivism: An early-twentieth-century school of philosophy that limits the scope of philosophy to the scientific method (empirical verification) and logic. Everything else philosophy once considered, such as metaphysics and ethics and theology, is tossed out the window as unverifiable and therefore meaningless.

Materialism: The philosophical position that there is only one thing in the universe: stuff, matter. Anything other than matter is either reducible to matter, as thoughts are reducible to the matter of a brain doing its thing, or doesn't exist, like the Tooth Fairy.

Metaphysics: One of the main topics of philosophy and a bit of a catchall for everything that isn't logic, epistemology, or ethics. Metaphysics looks at the Big Picture: What is "being"? What is the cosmos and what is it made of? Also, incidentally, what is the meaning of life?

Monism: The metaphysical position that ultimately the cosmos and everything in it is One Thing with a single unified set of natural laws that guide it. Saying that the entire universe is composed of only atoms that are managed by the universal laws of physics is a monistic statement. **Materialism** is a form of Monism.

Nihilism: Negativity as an approach to philosophy and life. Various types of Nihilism range from negating the existence of everything to negating the possibility of knowing anything to just negating social and political mores and morality in general. Not a reassuring philosophy. Always reminds me of King Lear's line, "Nothing will come of nothing."

Paradox: In logic, a statement or proposition that seems to be both true and false at the same time; a statement that internally contradicts itself. Bertrand Russell's model paradox asks, "Does the list of all lists that do not contain themselves contain itself?" If you say it does, then it doesn't, and vice versa. In human minds, paradoxes tend to cause cognitive dissonance, culminating in a chuckle.

Phenomenology: A philosophical discipline that studies subjective consciousness and how it is structured. Entire treatises have been written about the phenomenology of reading, the phenomenology of writing by hand, and the phenomenology of the memory of place. If all this sounds a lot like what self-conscious people do most of the time anyhow, you've got the idea.

Philogag: Neologism for a joke that explains or illuminates a philosophical concept. Also used to describe a philosophical concept that is funny in itself, as many paradoxes are.

Rationalism: In epistemology, the theory that truth begins and ends in the mind, not in the senses. It is the ultimate intellectualism, claiming that everything can be figured out deductively. For this to be so, reality has to have an intrinsically logical design; then all we have to do is really think about something and its nature will reveal itself right inside our beans.

Utilitarianism: A moral and political philosophy that proposes the doctrine of the greatest good/happiness for the greatest number of people. According to one of Utilitarianism's chief architects, Jeremy Bentham, the basic idea is to find a balance between the individual's happiness and the happiness of the community, "each counting in an equal way." In positing happiness as its aim, Utilitarianism is a type of hedonism.

Acknowledgments

A couple of years ago, I decided it was the right time to stop writing books. I wanted to devote my time to old man stuff—mostly relaxing and ruminating, along with spending more time with my friends and family. It was that ruminating part that drew me to my old "Pithies" notebook and to picking it up where I had left off decades earlier. When I told my friend and agent, Julia Lord, what I had been up to, she asked to take a look. She looked and suggested I make it into a book. All of which is to say that I cannot be trusted, even by myself. But thank you, Julia; I owe a lot to you.

I am also indebted to two friends who know a great deal more about philosophy than I do: my old pal Tom Cathcart and my new friend Warwick Fox, a retired professor of philosophy in Great Britain. Generously, both looked over my manuscript for mistakes, especially mistakes in reasoning. They not only found several, but they also offered ideas and examples of how to fix them. It is good to have friends who know more than I do.

Thanks also to my daughter, Samara, the first student of Judaica in my family in generations, who suggested I reference two of what she says are "the roughly nine things I know about the Talmud." And thanks, too, to Samara's partner, Daniel, a "Burner," for alerting me to the Timothy Leary essay.

As always, my wife, Freke Vuijst, went over my manuscript for mistakes in language and grammar. She found and corrected lots of them. I truly appreciate this even if it is embarrassing, considering that English is her second language.

I also thank Peter Cherneff for his reading and comments.

I am very fortunate to have such thoughtful, thorough, and encouraging editors at Penguin Books: Patrick Nolan, Emily Baker, and Max Reid. Thank you all.

I need to end here with something very sad for me. In the final weeks of my rewrites of this manuscript, my dog, Snookers, died of cancer. He was my dear friend and companion and, in many ways, my most persuasive teacher on the art of living well. I am deeply grateful to him for the years we spent together.